To You Through Me:
The Beginning of a Link of a Journey of 400 Years

Joe Minter

"THANK YOU GOD FOR THE HOLY GHOST FAITH VISION AND DREAM
IN 1989 TO BE A WORKER IN THIS VINEYARD BUILT BY YOUR HAND MY
LORD THY GOD IN LOVE AND PEACE TO OPEN THY CHILDREN EYES
AMAN."

-Joe Minter, painted on a sign at the entrance of the African Village in
America, Birmingham, Alabama

In the summer of 1989, Joe Minter had a vision from God to create art that
would honor the shared experiences of African Americans in this country.
Of more local concern, he had also heard that the city of Birmingham was
planning to build a civil rights museum and worried that the "foot soldiers"
would be left out of the official narrative. As a direct response, Minter began
building a sprawling collection of sculpture and installations on land adjacent
to both his home and the Shadow Lawn Memorial Gardens, a historically
black cemetery, in the Woodland Park neighborhood of Birmingham.
The result is a continuously evolving art environment that recounts both
immediately local and world events that have affected humanity, with a
focus on the contributions and tribulations of African Americans. The African
Village is completely constructed from materials that have been discarded,
a direct symbolic gesture reflecting the artist's belief that African-Americans
have themselves been discarded throughout American history. In Minter's
words, "The whole idea handed down to me by God is to use that which has
been discarded, just as we as a people have been discarded made invisible.
That what is invisible, thrown away, could be made into something so it
demonstrates that even what gets thrown away, with a spirit in it can survive
and grow. A spirit of all the people that has touched and felt that material
has stayed in the material. God supplies me with what is needed, what other
people throw away as junk, what I find on streets, and in flea markets, outlet
stores, Goodwill, Salvation Army. God gives me the messages to go on the
art, in the African Village in America."

In 2005, Minter produced the first edition of *To You Through Me: The
Beginning of a Link of a Journey of 400 Years*, a creative manifesto and
didactic field guide to his African Village in America yard show. Printed locally
and sold out of his home for $27.77, the publication walks the reader through
Minter's yard with images of site-specific installations that are supplemented
with prayers, maps, scripture, newspaper clippings, and charts. The works
are not organized chronologically or thematically. Instead, the publication
meanders through both the artist's yard and mind in an intuitive manner. The
book's design is equally improvisational. Designed by Minter, it incorporates
a variety of styles, fonts, and page layouts. The overall effect is one of
urgency and an expression of palpable need for the artist to share his original
vision, its basis in history and scripture, and the works that represent the
continuous fulfillment of that divine intervention.

On the thirtieth anniversary of his vision, Institute 193 and Tinwood have
re-issued *To You Through Me: The Beginning of a Link of a Journey of 400
Years.* It is our hope that those who cannot visit in person may use this first-
person guidebook to experience Joe Minter's yard and learn from his years
of thoughtful meditations on history, place, and the human condition.

-Phillip March Jones

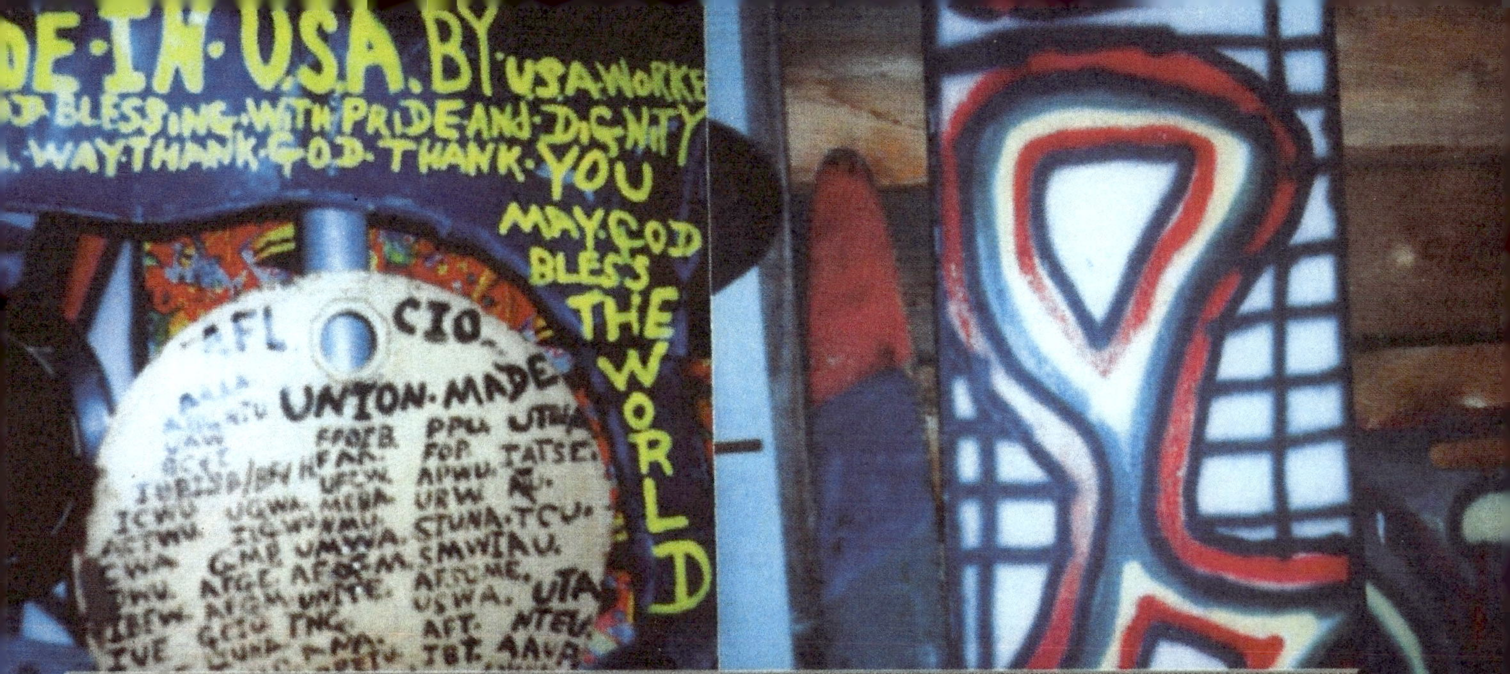

To You Through Me:

The Beginning of a Link of a Journey of 400 Years

by Joe Minter

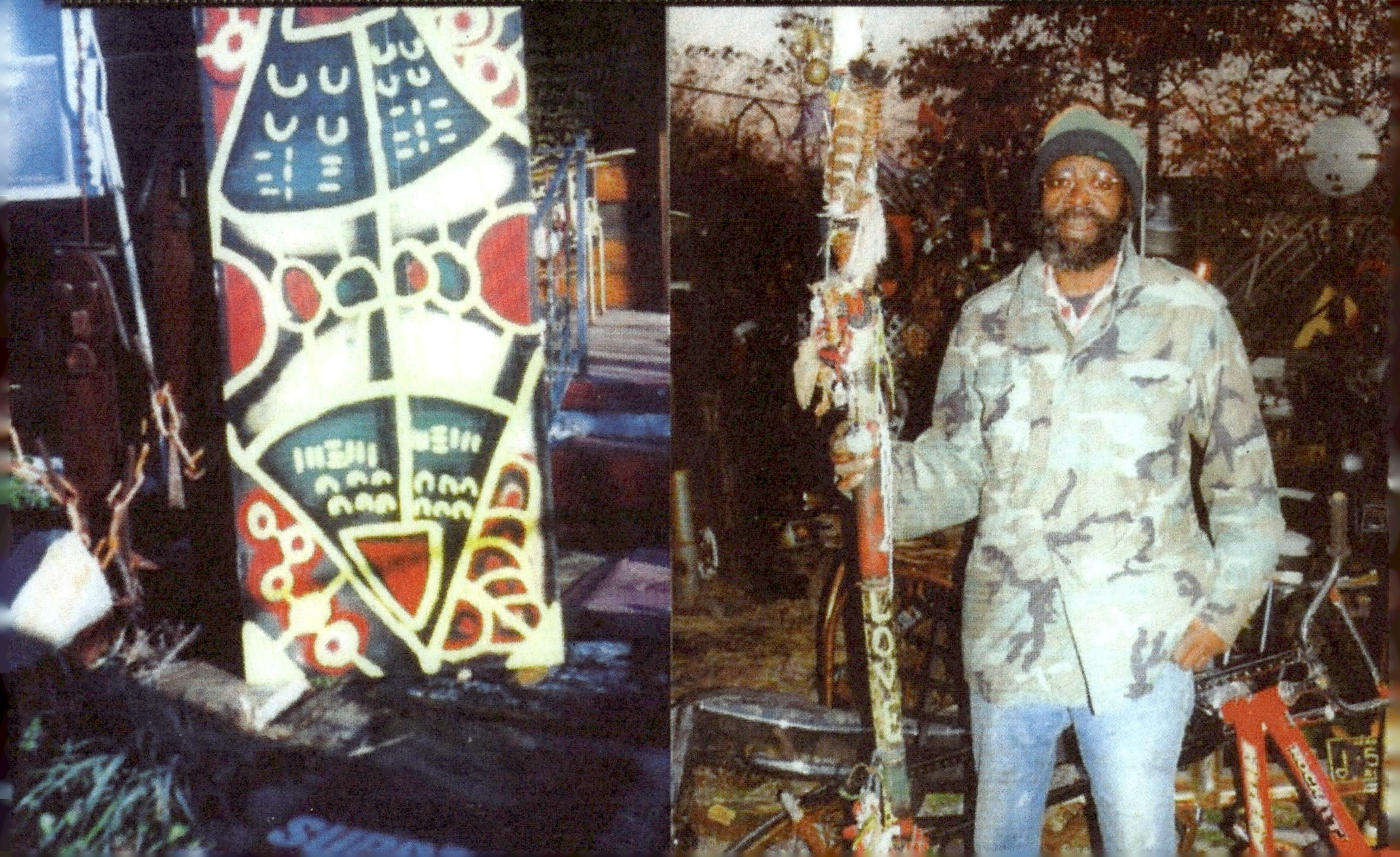

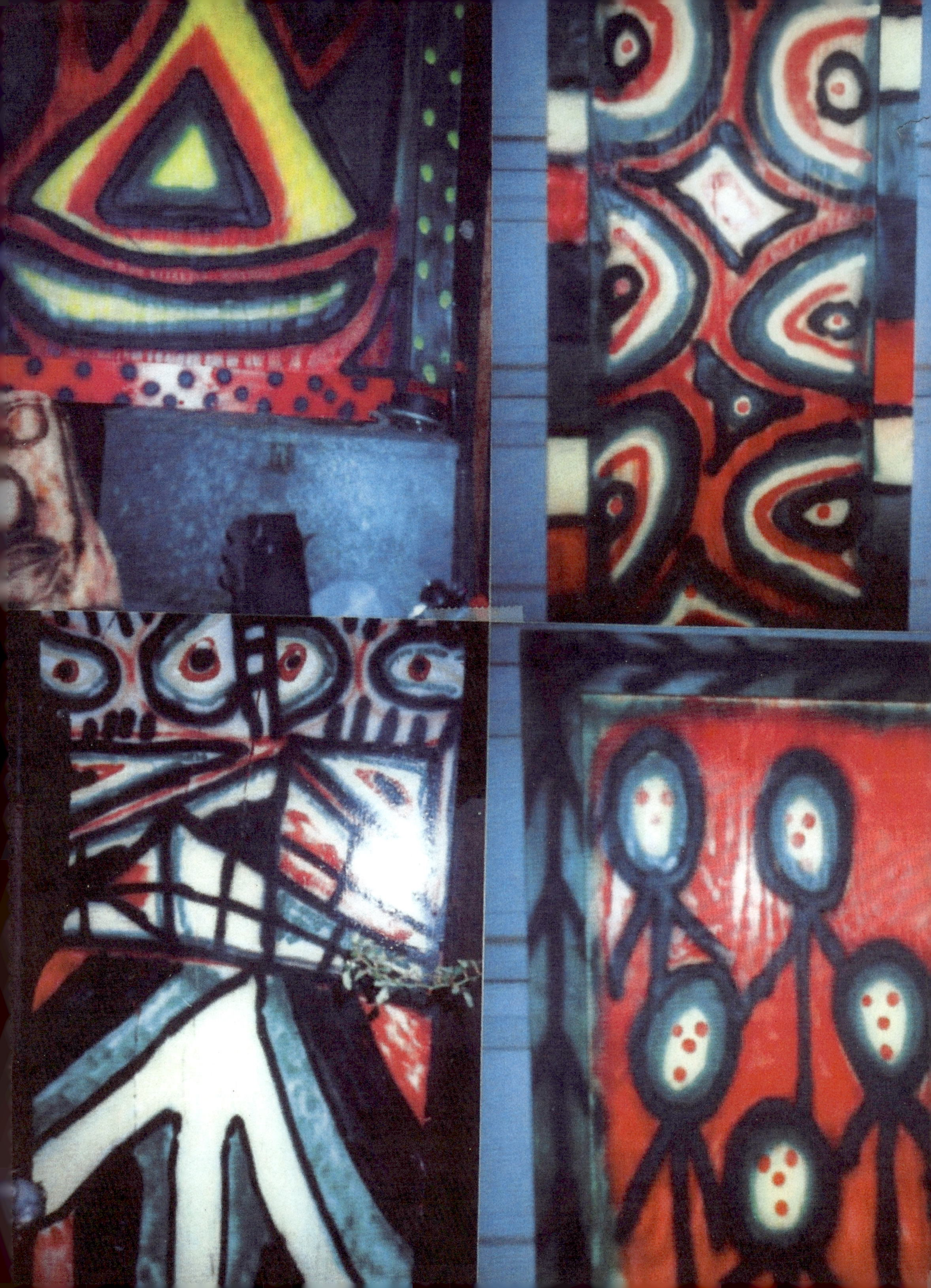

TO YOU THROUGH ME: THE BEGINNING OF A

LINK OF A JOURNEY

OF 400 YEARS

BY JOE MINTER SR.

CHAPTER 1

Today many of our youth do not know the contributions of African Americans to America other than their sweat and blood. In this first chapter there is a listing of all of our forgotten heroes that help make the United States what it is today.

<u>AFRICAN SERVICE IN U.S. WARS</u>

DURING THE AMERICAN REVOLUTION ABOUT 5,000 AFRICANS SERVED IN THE CONTINENTAL ARMY, MOSTLY IN INTEGRATED UNITS, AND SOME IN ALL AFRICAN COMBAT UNITS.

CIVIL WAR- 200,000 AFRICAN MEN SERVED IN THE UNION ARMY: 38,000 MEN WERE KILLED AND ONLY 22 OF THEM WON THE MEDAL OF HONOR (THE NATION'S HIGHEST AWARD).

WORLD WAR I- ABOUT 367,000 AFRICANS SERVED IN THE ARMED FORCES, 100,000 IN FRANCE.

WORLD WAR II- MORE THAN 1 MILLION AFRICANS SERVED IN THE ARMED FORCES: ALL-AFRICAN FIGHTER AND BOMBER AAF UNITS AND INFANTRY DIVISIONS GAVE DISTINGUISHED SERVICE. BY 1954, THE ARMED FORCES WERE COMPLETELY DESEGREGATED.

VIETNAM WAR- 274,937 AFRICANS SERVED IN THE ARMED FORCES (1965-74): 5,681 WERE KILLED IN COMBAT.

PERSIAN GULF WAR. ABOUT 104,000 AFRICANS SERVED IN THE KUWAITI THEATER -20% OF THE U.S. SOLDIERS, COMPARED WITH 8.7% FOR WORLD WAR II AND 9.8% FOR VIETNAM.

AFRICAN INVENTORS IN AMERICA

195 PATENTS WERE GRANTED FROM 1871 TO 1899

OVER 1,000 PATENTS WERE GRANTED TO AFRICANS BY 1913

A.J. BEARD 1897-JENNY COUPIER, 1892-ROTARY ENGINE

G.T. WOODS 1884-STEAM BOILER FURNACE, 1909-ELECTRIC RAILWAY,

1887- TELEGRAPHY, 1902-AIR BRAKES

R.B. SPIKERS 1932-AUTOMATIC GEAR SHIFT, 1933-TRANSMISSIONED SHIFT, 1940-

MULTIPLE BARREL MACHINE GUN

J. MATZELIGER 1891-AUTOMATIC SHOE LAST MACHINE

F.M. JONES 1949-AIR CONDITION UNIT & REFRIGERATED TRUCK, 1957-

REFRIGERATED BOX CAR, 1950-2-CYCLE GAS ENGINE

E.J. MCCOY 1872-AUTOMATIC LUBRICATORS 50 DIFFERENT UNITS AND 25 OTHER

MECHANICAL DEVICES

J. STANDARD 1889-OIL STOVE 1891-REFRIGERATOR
R.F. FLEMMING JR. 1886-GUITAR
J. GREGORY 1886-MOTOR
A.P. ASHBOURNE 1880-PROCESSED COCONUT OIL
MORE THAN 1,500 AFRICANS CONTRIBUTED TO AMERICAN SCIENCE AND MEDICINE
BOOK BY VIVIAN SAMMONS CESAR (SLAVE) MEDICINE PRACTIONER FOUND CURE
FOR RATTLE SNAKE BITE IN 1700
C.R. DREW PHYSICIAN/SURGEON FOUNDED A BLOOD BANK 1904-1970

B.O. DAVIS SR. WAS THE 1ST AFRICAN GENERAL IN THE UNITED STATES ARMY-1940

B.O. DAVIS JR. WAS THE 1ST AFRICAN GENERAL IN THE UNITED STATES AIR FORCE

1954

MARY ELIZABETH MAHONEY (1845-1926) WAS THE 1ST AFRICAN AMERICAN NURSE

TO GRADUATE IN THE UNITED STATES. HER ACHIEVEMENTS ARE STILL HONORED

TODAY THROUGH THE MARY MAHONEY MEDAL WHICH IS AWARDED BY THE

AMERICAN NURSES ASSOCIATION EVERY TWO YEARS.

H.O. FLIPPER 1ST AFRICAN GRADUATE OF USMA WEST POINT 2ND LT. REGULAR

ARMY CALVARY IN 1879

R. ARRINGTON JR. ZOOLOGIST 1934

GEORGE WASHINGTON CARVER (1864-1943) AGRICULTURIST THAT DEVELOPED

THE SWEET POTATO, THE PEANUT, AND THE SOY BEAN.

B. BANNEKER (1731-1806) SURVEYOR

W.A. RAYFIELD ARCHITECT

<u>AFRICAN ASTRONAUTS</u>

G.S. BLUFORD JR., C.S. BOLDEN, E.J. DWIGHT, F. D. GREGORY, M.C. JEMISON, R.H.

LAWRENCE, R.E. MCNAIR

TUSKEEGEE AIRMEN 332ND, 99TH PURSUE SQUADRON-WORLD WAR II,

555TH PARACHUTE INFANTRY

TRIPLE NICKELS 1943-1992

INTRODUCTION

Awake my beloved children of Africa and praise the Lord thy God. How did our first ancestors survive the middle passage and diaspora across the Atlantic Ocean to the Americas and Europe, the burial waters of millions of our African ancestors. They were chained and shackled in the belly of thousands of ships and forced into a lifetime of slavery, they lost their freedom, had to deal with a lifetime of misery and agony sent down from generation to generation. God was with us and always will be. The African has struggled here in America for 400 years in order to be free. All we have received from America is a lot of broken promises. Our struggle for freedom and to be treated equally is not over yet. We must fight, believe we can surpass it, and stick together as a people.

It is God's will for all of his beloved children to be free. We as descendents of Africa that were free in the motherland, must recognize the struggle our forefathers and ancestors went through and press on. Both the American and European economies were built from the free labor of the African American. Our race has been exploited and stripped of its own lands natural resources.

I am a descendent of the first free African that was made into slaves by America and Europe. The Atlantic was a trail of death for millions of our African ancestors. There were thousands of sharks that circled the ships awaiting food. That food was the African body thrown overboard. There was a number of types of torture handed to us in the form of starvation, beatings, slaves laid in vomit from other slaves, feces, and some were thrown overboard because the captain wanted them to be tossed. Some slaves tried to escape and swim back to the motherland, most of which were unsuccessful. The captain and crewmen of the ship had the nerve to call themselves Christians. The slave trade was not what Jesus wanted. No one can stop the will of God, Americans, nor Europeans. God will carry us back into the warm breast of our treasured motherland of Africa and we will be able to say free at last,

free at last, thank God almighty we are free at last. Praise the Lord thy God.

A child of God
Joe Minter Sr.
Peacemaker

P.S. This is a story of a people that is African and no one can explain the facts like an African. We have built and served America all of our lives. We have been made invisible in a land that is full of Christian beliefs who continue to look upon their brothers and sisters as less than human beings if they are of African decent. I pray that my words will touch many hearts in America and in Europe and the whole world turn one day as Jesus did to save our sins and forgive one another and love one another equally. I pray that this excerpt will not fall on deaf ears. This might be our last change to come together as one in love for one another. We may not have it all together, but together we have it all.

Since my people were extracted from our mother land of Africa, we have been oppressed and

misused by the white man. As a people we have suffered every inhuman injustice there is on earth. I

cannot see how one man calls himself a Christian, can treat a fellow man as if he was inhuman. All of

us were born in the image of God. Our white fellow man seems to over look this. We were brought

over by force, being separated from our family, for more reason other than to be a slave. In the country

we don't belong in and the white man stole we all are intrudes upon a land all ready inhabited by the

true people that God put here, the American Indian. The American Indian was the one who was not

here to mutilate the land but to preserve it. One who took from the land only the bear necessity required

to live. It seems that this is a world where man is against man, if it wasn't like this there would be no

strong or weak. If this system had no strong or weak people there would no being. For this is how we

exist, and in existing there are those on the weak side that suffer and those on the strong side that suffer.

The strong have come a long way. The weak have come right along with them. It seems that the strong

can't get rid of the other. Because of the weak and strong there is also a dislike for each other. Hate is a small word but is the reason there is so much trouble in the world today. Hate is what put race against

race. There were laws passed to preserve the nation and the government. These laws preserved some

form of order but they still kept the people fighting among themselves. Because whenever the law

helps some, it handicaps others. Where laws are passed to help one race of people; another race of

people will dislike the law and there is a bitter disagreement. If the people just stop and think, while we

are fighting and trying to kill each other we would be better off all the way around. If we work at same

places and children go to the same school we might as well learn to live together because we can't

THE VISION

2004

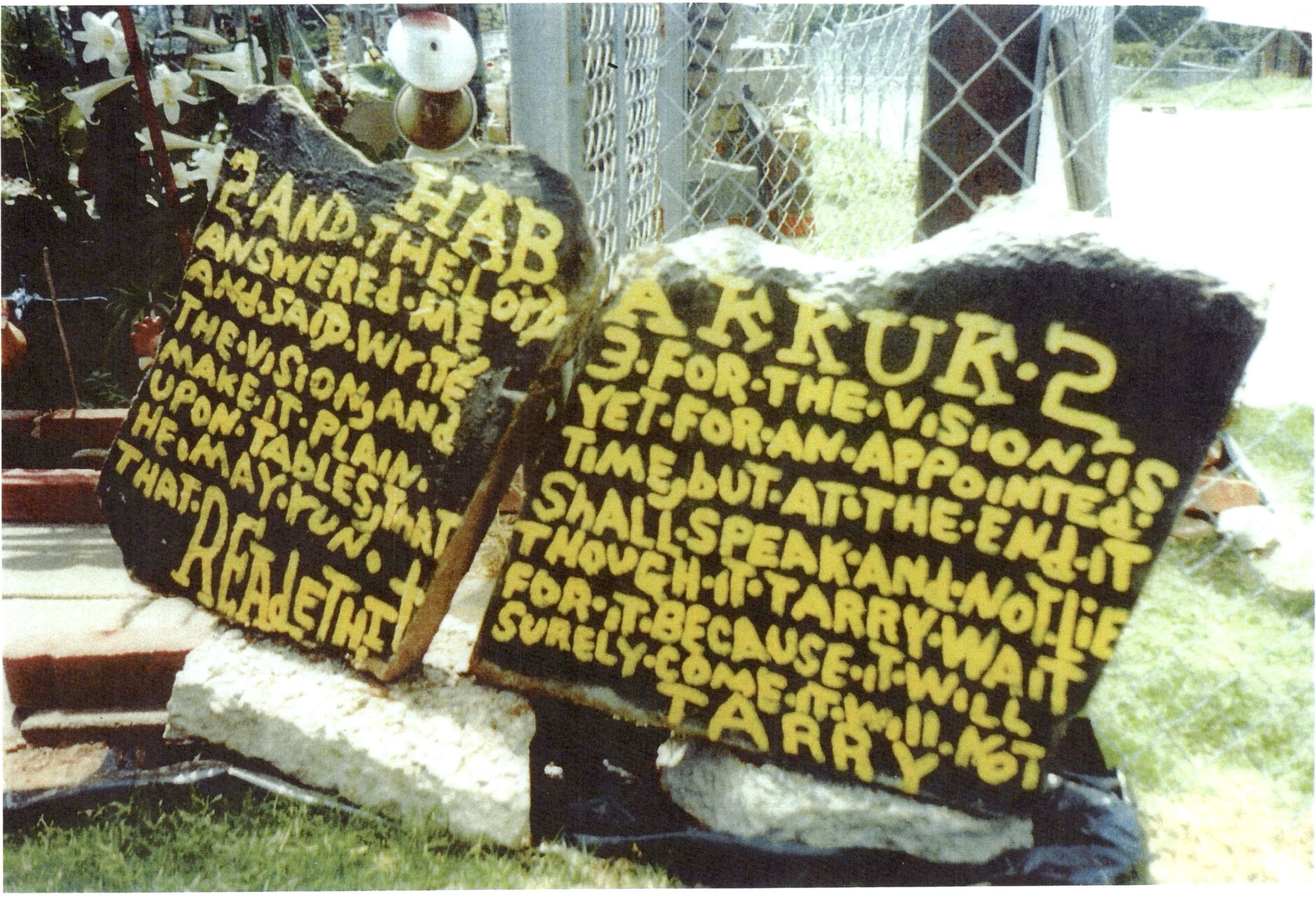

HAB
2. AND THE LORD
ANSWERED ME
AND SAID WRITE
THE VISION AND
MAKE IT PLAIN
UPON TABLES THAT
HE MAY RUN
THAT READETH IT
AKKUR 2
3. FOR THE VISION IS
YET FOR AN APPOINTED
TIME BUT AT THE END IT
SHALL SPEAK AND NOT LIE
THOUGH IT TARRY WAIT
FOR IT BECAUSE IT WILL
SURELY COME IT WILL NOT
TARRY

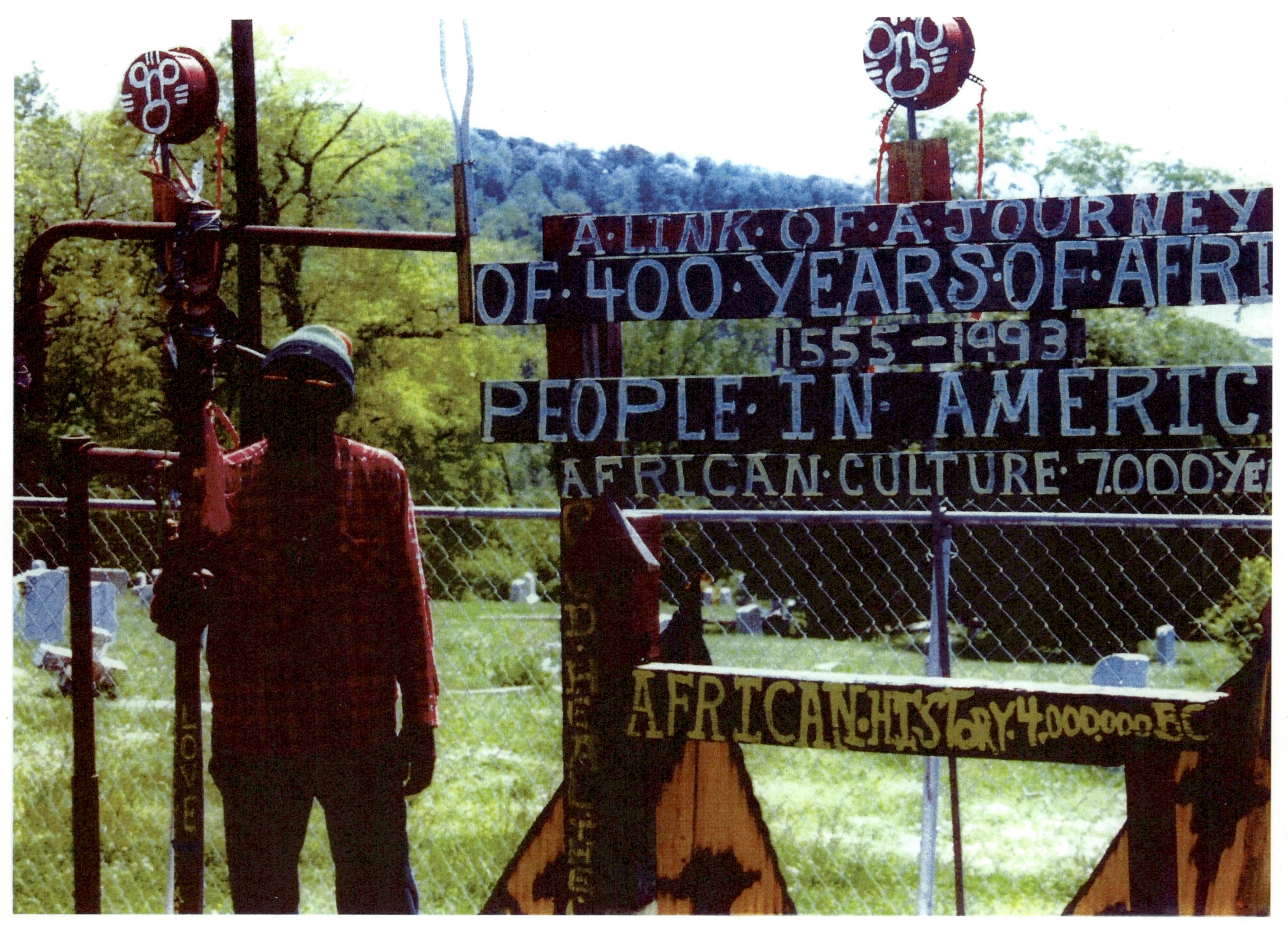

A·LINK·OF·A·JOURNEY
OF·400·YEARS·OF·AFRI
1555 - 1993
PEOPLE·IN·AMERIC
AFRICAN·CULTURE·7000·YE
AFRICAN·HISTORY·4,000,000·BC
LOVE

get anywhere trying to hold one another down. We can't get anywhere trying to stop the progress of the world because it will roll over you and keep right on going. All of us are human beings, we just differ by race. Just because a man of a different race moves into a neighborhood, how is it that someone would pack up their belongings and drag their family to yet another neighborhood? You should stay and try to love and understand one another. Many try to run but cannot escape reality. We have given our best to the world. It seems that people on this earth can't seem to see that we have been through it and we are still laying everything on the line in order to get all the rights and benefits all Americans are insured. In the law of the land I cannot see what makes one American run from another American. Africans make up a large part of the American history, yet were left out of it. We are a progressive race of people. If one uses common sense, the past speaks for itself through the actions of the African people. We have come a very long way but not far enough to stop. It took my people a long time to find themselves. But we have looked into the mirror and know who we are; a proud people close to God. God has brought us through many hardships and the way we bare our hardships is through song. We are not a race of people who are inferior but a race that leads the way. We can make a way out of no way. We are but a race who has been exploited by the white man. The white man can't take away our culture and from this we can sprout many new roots. We have found that things we thought were not in us have been in us all the while. Only in this day and time has it been exposed. We can look at the shape and conditions that we are in now and imagine what despair our forefathers had to go through. We have come from a sapling and grown into a tree. Although we have lost many beautiful branches

JOE & HILDA

A LINK OF A JOURNEY OF 400 YEARS OF

AFRICAN PEOPLE LOST IN AMERICA

1993

and leaves, the tree is still standing as strong as ever. The determination of the youth of our race has lit

a spark in the old for they are tired of lying down and dying as well.

CHAPTER 2

I HAVE FOUND AS A BLACK MAN THAT A WHITE MAN USES WORDS LIKE WHITE SUPREMACY WHICH IS MISLEADING. FROM THIS WORD WHITE SUPREMACY, STEMS SUCH WORDS AS HATE, BIGOT, BIAS, AND SEGREGATION. ALL BLACK PEOPLE COME IN CONTACT WITH THESE WORDS EVERYDAY OF THEIR LIVES. WE HAVE TO BE (3 TIMES BETTER) TRIPLE BETTER THAN THE NEXT WHITE MAN TO GET THE JOB. THE ADVANTAGE JOB THAT A BLACK MAN GETS A LOT OF PRESSURE IS BEHIND IT. THIS IS WITH A WHITE MAN STANDING OVER HIM LIKE HE IS A PRISONER, BECAUSE HE IS A BLACK MAN AND HE IS TRYING TO GET HIM TERMINATED WITH EVERY TRICK HE CAN THINK OF. THE CIVIL RIGHTS ACTS GAVE THE BLACK MAN SOMETHING TO FIGHT BACK WITH, BUT IT DIDN'T CHANGE THE WHITE MAN AT ALL. YES I AM BLACK AND PROUD OF IT. WE HAVE PROVED WE ARE TRULY AMERICAN. WE CAN'T BE SWEPT UNDR THE RUG LIKE DIRT. UNLIKE THE WHITE MAN, THE BLACK MAN HAS GIVEN ALL THAT HE CAN GIVE AND EVEN MORE. YOU CAN'T KEEP A MAN IN THE GUTTER WITHOUT GETTING INTO THE GUTTER YOURSELF. THIS IS WHAT THE WHITE MAN TRIED TO DO TO THE BLACK MAN BUT IT DIDN'T WORK. THE WHITE MAN ISN'T THE ONLY MAN ON EARTH WHO CAN GO TO COLLEGE AND GET A DEGREE. THE BLACK MAN GOES TO COLLEGE ALSO, EVEN THOUGH HE HAS TO WORK HIS WAY THROUGH IT. THIS PUT A LOT OF PRESSURE ON HIM BUT HE IS CAPABLE OF EARNING A DEGREE. HE THEN HAS TO GET A JOB TO TRY TO PAY BACK SOME OF HIS DEBTS HE ACCUMULATED WHILE WORKING HIS WAY THROUGH COLLEGE. THE AVERAGE WHITE MAN HAS PARENTS TO SEND THEIR CHILDREN TO COLLEGE. THE CHILDREN DON'T EVEN HAVE TO CHOOSE A MAJOR IN COLLEGE UNTIL THEY GET READY AND THE PARENTS PAYS THE WHOLE BILL. SOME PARENTS EVEN BUY THEIR CHILDREN A NEW CAR. WE AS A PEOPLE HAVE A LOT OF

PRIDE IN OUR CHILDREN. FOR WE HAVE NOT STAYED AWAY FROM THEM. FOR WE HAVE GIVEN THEM LOVE, TRUST AND A SENSE OF KNOWING WHO THEY ARE. WE HAVE NOT BEEN TOO PROUD TO NEAL ON OUR KNEES AND PRAY WHEN TIMES GET HARD. THIS THAT WE HAVE BEEN GIVEN TO US WAS NOT ON A SILVER PLATTER. WE ARE CALLED TROUBLE MAKERS, AGITATES, MILITANT, COMMUNIST, AND MANY MORE NAMES THAT HAVE LABLED US FOR NO REASON AT ALL. FOR WE DIN'T MAKE THE TROUBLE THE TROUBLE WAS MADE WHEN WE AS A PEOPLE WERE CHAINED AND SHACKELED AND DRIVEN FROM OUR MOTHER LAND. IT WAS LIKE A HERD OF CATTLE HEADED FOR THE SLAUGHTER PEN. WE DIDN'T FORCE OURSELVES ON THIS COUNTRY. THIS COUNTRY FORCED ITSELF ON US. WE HAVE CARRIED OUR LOAD OF THE BURDEN OF THIS COUNTRY FOR A LONG TIME AND HAVE RECEIVED NOTHING FOR IT IN RETURN. THIS IS 1976, BUT WE ARE TREATED LIKE IT IS 1876. I ONLY FEEL HATE, BIGOTRY, DISCRIMINATION, AND INJUSTICE. FOR AS MUCH HEARTACHE AND HURT THE BLACK RACE HAS GONE THROUGH, WHEN WILL OUR COUNTRY REALIZE OUR PAIN AND SUFFERING. WHEN WE ARE CALLED TO SERVE IN THE ARMED FORCES, WE GO. WHEN IT IS ALL OVER IT IS THE BLACK RACE WHO ARE SILL LEFT IN THE COLD WITH NO WHERE TO GO. HOW COULD A FREE COUNTRY BORN FROM A DEMOCRACY INSLAVE ANOTHER HUMAN BEING. THIS IS WHAT HAPPENS TO THE BLACK RACE. FOR WE AS A PEOPLE HAD OUR CIVILIZATION, OUR OWN CULTURE, AND OUR OWN COUNTRY. THIS COUNTRY DIDN'T WANT THE BLACK RACE TO EVEN LEARN TO READ AND WRITE. WE LEARNED AND IT COSTED OUR RACE MANY LIVES. A COUNTRY WHO'S ROOTS IS THE CONSTITUTIONS OF THE UNITED STATES AND OF THE LAND. THE BILL OF RIGHTS AND MANY OTHER LAWS MADE BY MAN. ALL OF THESE LAWS FOR A FREE COUNTRY YET

THEY STILL DIDN'T MAKE THE BLACK MAN FREE. MANY BLACKS HAVE DIED TO BE FREE BUT WE ARE NOT FREE YET.

EACH DAY WE GO FOR THE LIKE A WARRIOR INTO BATTLE WITH NOTHING TO PROTECT US WITH BUT OUR LOVE AND BELIEF IN GOD. FOR NOT MATTER HOW FAR YOU GO WE NEED HIM EVERY MINUTE AND EVERY HOUR OF EVERY DAY. I HAVE FOUND OUT THAT IF YOU HELP YOURSELF HE WILL LEAD THE WAY ALL THE WAY. IT IS HARD FOR ME AS A MAN TO WORK EVERYDAY SIDE BY SIDE ANOTHER MAN AND HE NOT FULLY COMMUNICATE WITH ME BECAUSE I AM OF A DIFFERENT COLOR THAN HE. WE ALL WERE MADE OF ONE IMAGE. MY PEOPLE SHOULD NOT BE AN OUTCAST BECAUSE OF OUR COLOR. FOR GOD MADE THE RAINBOW AND TRULY THIS WASN'T BY CHANCE. IT TAKES ALL COLORS TO REFLECT ALL OF GOD'S GLORY FOR MAN TO SEE. I HAVE TO STAND AS A MAN FOR MY CHILDREN TO KNOW MYSELF AS A MAN. FOR THIS MY LIFE WILL NOT BE IN VAIN. A MAN SHOULD STAND AS TALL AS A PINE TREE, TOUGH AS AN OAK YET GENTLE AS A WILLOW TREE IN A SUNNY SPRING DAY BLOWING IN THE WIND. THERE IS NOT HARM IN A MAN WHO LET THE WORLD KNOW THAT HE KNOWS HOW TO SMILE AND HOW TO SHED A TEAR, OR HOW TO BRING JOY TO EVERYONE AND EVERYTHING THAT HE COMES INTO CONTACT WITH. FOR A MAN IS KNOW FOR THE SHALLOW THAT HE CAST SO EVERYONE CAN SEE YOU AND THE GOODNESS THAT YOU SPREAD FOR THIS GOODNESS WILL TOUCH EVERYONE. GIVE OFF A RAY OF LOVE, A RAY OF HAPPINESS, A RAY OF UNDERSTANDING, AND A RAY OF JOY. ALL OF THIS WILL MAKE YOUR HEART FEEL LIKE IT IS ABOUT TO BURST. WALK AND TALK WITH PEOPLE NOT ONLY YOUR AGE, BUT THINK ABOUT THE CHILDREN, FOR THEY ARE LIKE A CUP THAT HAS TO BE FILLED. TRY TO HELP SOMEONE EACH AND EVERYDAY OF YOUR LIFE

BECAUSE IN THE LONG RUN THIS WILL PAY OFF. TRY TO FIND OUT ABOUT THINGS AROUGN YOU THAT NATURE HAS PERFECT FOR YOU. FOR WHEN GOD MADE YOU HE DIDN'T WANT HIS SENSES THAT HE GAVE TO YOU TO GO TO WASTE BECAUSE IF THIS WAS THE CASE HE WOULD NOT HAVE GIVEN THEM TO YOU THIS IS TRULY A BLESSING.

IT SEEMS TO ME THAT JUST TO BE A BLACK MAN IS TRULY AN EXPERIENCE THAT CAN ONLY BE FELT BY ME WITHIN MYSELF. I GO TO WORK BECAUSE I HAVE A FAMILY LIKE MANY MEN HAVE. I TRY WITH ALL MY HEART AND SOUL TO TRY TO WORK AS HARD AS I CAN AND HAVE A GOOD ATTENDANCE RECORD. THIS ISN'T ENOUGH FOR THE WHITE MAN BECAUSE HE MAKES A MOCKERY OF THIS. FOR WHEN YOU MAKE YOUR FIRST MISTAKE HE IS THERE TO TRY TO CRUSH YOU INTO THE GROUND. THROUGH ALL OF THIS A BLACK MAN FINDS THE STRENGTH IN HIS SOUL TO CARRY ON FOR HIS FAMIL. THIS TO ME MAKES A REAL MAN. FOR WITHIN ME IS THE HURT, THE JOY, THE HAPPINESS THE FEAR, THE LOVE, THE DESPAIR AND TO KNOW THE TRUE MEANING OF GRACE. THE LIFE OF A BLACK MAN IS LIKE BEING IN A SPIDER WEB AS LARGE AS THE WORLD. I HAVE BEEN ON THIS EARTH 35 YEARS AND I HAVE YET TO ESCAPE THIS WEB. IT LOOKS TO ME LIKE THE OLDER YOU GET THE LARGER THE WEB BECOMES. IT IS A HURTFUL FEELING WHEN YOU WORK AS HARD AS YOU CAN ON A JOB FOR TEN YEARS AND IT IS ALL UP HILL CLIMBING. TAKE THE BITTER WITH THE SWEET. WHEN YOU FEEL IT IS TIME TO MAKE ONE STEP UP AND TRY TO BETTER YOURSELF FOR YOUR FAMILY, YOU GET KNOCKED BACK DOWN AGAIN. FOR IN ONE DAY A COMPANY CAN DESTROY TEN

YEARS OF HARD EARNED SENIORITY, AND REDUCE YOU TO THE LOWEST SENIOR JOB IN THE PLANT. THIS DOESN'T JUST HAPPEN IN ONE PLANT; IT HAPPENS EVERYWHERE. THIS IS PART OF THE LEGACY OF BEING A BLACK MAN AND LIVING A LIFE THAT YOU KNOW YOU HAVE TO FIGHT EVERYDAY OF YOUR NATURAL BORN LIFE. WE FIGHT BUT WE CAN'T FALL FOR IF WE DO THIS WILL BE THE END OF THE BLACK MAN AND WE WILL BECOME EXTINCT. THIS WILL NOT HAPPEN. THE WORLD AS WE KNOW IT WILL BE NO MORE, FOR GOD WILL NEVER FORSAKE HIS CHILDREN THIS I BELIEVE WITH ALL MY HEART AND ALL MY SOUL.

WE MAY FEEL THAT WE ARE AT OUR END AND JUST LOOK BACK AND SEE HOW FAR WE AS A PEOPLE AND A RACE HAVE COME. THIS DIDN'T HAPPEN BECAUSE WE MADE IT HAPPEN THIS IS THE WAY GOD WANTED IT TO HAPPEN. ALL YOU HAVE TO DO IS LOOK AROUND SEE. MAN HAS NO CONTROL OVER FIRE, WATER, OR WIND. THESE ARE JUST COMMON THINGS YOU CAN LOOK AT AND SEE. MAN HAS NO POWER. ITS ALL IN THE HAND OF GOD. GOD HAS POWER OVER THESE AND EVERY MAN AND THINGS THAT EXIST ON THE FACE OF THE EARTH. WE MIGHT BE HUNGRY OR WITHOUT A JOB BUT GOD IS THE ONE WHO HOLDS ALL OF THIS IN HIS HANDS. FOR IT IS A LOT TO BE LEARNED BY THE WORDS "MAN SHOULD NOT LIVE BY BREAD ALONE." FOR WITHIN THIS IT IS A LOT THAT COMES BEFORE THE BREAD. MAN HAS NEVER SOTPPED AND LOOKED AT ALL OF THE THINGS AROUND HIM AND ACKNOWLEDGE ALL OF THIS BLESSINGS. FOR AL OF THESE THE SMALL AS WELL AS THE LARGE CAN BE TAKEN AWAY FROM HIM. WHEN GOD MADE THE WORLD HE MADE IT SO ALL OF US COULD LIVE IN PEACE, LOVE, AND IN UNDERSTANDING OF ONE ANOTHER. BUT MAN IS TRYING TO ROB THE EARTH OF THE RICHES GOD PUT INTO HIS BEAUTIFUL EARTH. WITH THIS YOU FIND THE RICH

TAKING FROM THE EARTH ALL THAT IT HAS AND OVER LOOKING THE POOR PEOPLE WHO HAVE NO WHERE TO GO BUT FOR WHAT MAN TAKE OUT OF THE EARTH HE CAN'T REPLACE. ONLY GOD CAN REPLACE THIS THAT MAN HAS DESTROYED. IT IS TIME TO STOP DESTROYING AND START REBUILDING. IF WE DO NOT, OUR WHOLE HUMAN RACE WILL BE DESTROYED. FOR IF GOD WANTED TO LET HIS EARTH REMAIN AS HE MADE IT HE WOULD NOT HAVE PUT MAN HERE AS A CARETAKER. HE DID NOT INTEND FOR US TO DESTROY AND GET RICH FROM THE EARTH BUT TO PRESERVE IT AND TAKE ONLY FROM IT THAT WHICH WAS NEEDED TO IVE. FOR WITH ALL THE LIVING THINGS GOD PUT ON EARTH, ONLY MAN IS DESTROYING AND EVERYTHING ALONG WITH IT. IT IS VERY BAD FOR ME TO VIEW A COUNTRY WITH SUCH RICH, POWERS AND OPPORTUNITY WITH ENOUGH TO TAKE CARE OF THE WHOLE WORLD; TO BECOME A CONTRY OF THE HAVE AND THE HAVE NOTS. FOR IT SEEMS THAT THE RICH ARE IN POER AND THERE IS NO NEED FOR THE POOR, THE CHILDREN, OR THE OLD PEOPLE. NOT EVEN THE FARMERS OR THE ONES WHO PUT THE BREAD IN THE RICH MAN'S MOUTH AS WELL AS THE POOR MAN'S. FOR SOME REASON WE SEEM TO BE IN A STATE OF DEGENRATION. FOR WE AS A COUNTRY AND AS A PEOPLE HAVE LOST THE SENSE OF WHO AND WHAT WE ARE AND WHERE WE ARE GOING. THIS ISN'T ONLY AFFECTING THE BLACK RACE, CUT ALL THE RACES' IN AMERICA. THE THING THAT IS KILLING US IS THE RICH MAN FASCINATING WITH TECHNOLOGY AND A GOVENRMENT THAT CAN BE CALLED A TECHNOCRACY. THIS IS WHAT IS GOING TO BE THE DOWN FALL OF US ALL BECAUSE IN A TECHNOLOGY BASED SOCIETY MAN ISN'T NEEDED. THIS IS THE END OF ALL THE JOBS THAT MEN NOW HAVE. IT IS TIME FOR EVERY MAN, WOMAN, AND CHILD TO LOOK ALL AROUND AND SEE WHICH DIRECTION WE ARE GOING. IT SEEMS TO BE THE ROAD TO

ARMAGEDDON. IT IS ALSO TIME FOR ALL OF US TO CHANGE THIS DIRECTION, BUT IN ORDER TO DO THIS, WE ALL AS A HUMAN RACE MUST COME TOGETHER. WHEN THIS TIME COMES, (WHICH IS NOW) YOU CAN SAY GOODBYE TO THE RICH AND THE POOR, THE WALL STREETS OR THE NO STREETS, THE GHETTOS, THE SUBURBS, THE BLACK AND WHITE. THE WHITE MAN IS SO BUSY BULLDOZING THE BLACK MAN INTO THE GROUND THAT HE FORGOT TO CHECK HIS BACK AND FORTH HIS SIDES. BECAUSE THINGS ARE CLOSING IN ON HIM, HE IS TRYING TO BURY THE BLACK MAN. THE WHITE MAN DOESN'T REALIZE THAT THE BLACK MAN MADE HIM WHAT HE IS TODAY. FOR EACH THING THAT HAS BEEN DONE BY THE WHITE MAN WAS TAKEN FROM THE IDEALS AND THE WISDOM OF A BLACK MAN.

OUR COUNTRY KNOWN AS THE UNITED STATES OF AMERICA, OR "WHITE MAN'S COUNTRY," IS HEADED DOWN HILL. ALMIGHTY GOD IS ABOUT TO APPEAR IN AND ALL AROUND THIS COUNTRY. HOW IS IT ONE CAN PREACH THE WHOLE BIBLE AND BE ONE OF THE BIGGEST HYPOCRITES IN THE WORLD? FOR YOU CANNOT LIVE BY MAN MADE LAWS OR DO UNTO YOUR FELLOW MAN AS YOU WOULD HAVE HIM DO UNTO YOU. YU HAVE TO KNOW THE LAWS OF GOD AND LIVE BY THEM EVERYDAY OF YOUR LIFE. FOR THERE IS ONLY TEN LAWS OF GOD. "THE TEN COMMANDMENTS." FOR GOD GAVE THESE TO ALL HIS CHILDREN IN ORDER TO LIVE A FULL LIFE. A LIFE OF PEACE AND OF FULLFILLMENT AND FOR PEACE ON EARTY AND GOOD WILL TOWARD MEN. EVERYONE ON EARTH CAN LIVE IN A STATE OF LOVE ALL OVER THE WORLD IF THE WHITE MAN OBEYED THESE COMMANDMENTS OF GOD. FOR I KNOW AS A BLACK MAN THAT WE KNOW WHO GOD IS. HE WALKS WITH US EVERYDAY.
EVERYDAY OF OUR LIVES WE KNOW THESE COMMANDMENTS AND THEY TRY WITH ALL OF THEIR HEARTS AND SOULS TO KEEP THIS IN OUR HEARTS. THAT ENABLES A BLACK MAN TO SMILE WHEN ALL OF THE WORLD IS AGINST HIM BECAUSE OF THE WHITE MAN. I ALWAYS REMEMBER THAT A BLACK MAN NEVER WALKS ALONE BECAUSE GOD IS ALWAYS WITH HIM. FOR GOD SO LOVED THE BLACK THAT HE GAVE HIM A WAY TO COMMUNICATE ALL OVER THE WORLD AND BE WELL HEARD AND UNDERSTOOD. THROUGH THIS ALL THE BLACK MAN'S FEELINGS, HARDSHIPS, GOOD TIMES, AND LOVE FOR GOD AND HIS FELLOW MAN COULD BE FULLY EXPRESSED. THIS IS THE BLACK MAN'S MUSIC. FOR TO HEAR THE BLACK MAN SING IT IS GOD'S GIFT TO HIM TO LET HIM KNOW THAT GOD'S LOVES ALL OF HIS CHILDREN ALL THE TIME. HE WANTS TO LEAVE HIM ALONE TO FIGHT THIS EVIL IN THE WORLD ALL BY HIMSELF. GOD MADE A BLACK MAN AND PUT HIM IN A GARDEN OF EDEN WHICH IS KNOWN TO THE WORLD AS AFRICA AND ALSO KNOWN FOR MANY YEARS BY THE WHITE MAN AS THE DARK CONTINENT BECAUSE HE DIDN'T UNDERSTAND IT. HE DIDN'T UNDERSTAND THE

PEOPLE EITHER. MAN DID NOT UNDERSTAND THIS WONDERFUL LAND OR ITS BEAUTIFUL PEOPLE. GOD MADE IN HIS OWN IMAGE OF THIS TODAY. FOR THIS REASON THE WHITE MAN CAME TO AFRICA ON SHIPS TO CAPTURE AND ENSLAVE GOD'S CHILDREN: THE BLACK MAN. THE WHITE MAN ALSO WANTED TO RUN A RAMPAGE ON THIS GARDEN OF EDEN WHICH GOD MADE BY HIS OWN HANDS. THE WHITE MAN WANTED TO RULE IT WITH THE POWER OF HIS GUN NOT THE POWER OF GOD. THE WHITE MAN HAS NO FEAR OF GOD; IF SO, HE WOULD LIVE BY HIS COMMANDMENTS. YOU CAN NOT HOLD THE HOLY BIBLE IN ONE HAND AND A MACHINE GUN IN THE OTHER AND IF YOU HOLD THE BIBLE IN BOTH HANDS AND GO ALONG WITH THE MAN HOLDING THE WEAPON AND THE BIBLE, YOU ARE A MUCH BIGGER HYPOCRITE THAN HE. FOR THE BLACK MAN HAS TURNED EVERYDAY IN THE WORLD AND IN EVERYWAY. FOR NOW THE BLACK MAN IS ABOUT TO CRY OUT IN THE WILDERNESS WHICH IS THE WORLD WHICH IS COMPLETELY CONTROLLED BY WHITE MEN. I PRAY TO GOD IN HEAVEN TO STOP THIS HAVOC AND THE ENSLAVEMENT OF HIS CHILDREN EVEN TODAY. FOR HE WHO SITS HIGH AND LOOKS LOW IS THE ONLY ONE WHO CAN STOP THIS. I AM A BLACK MAN AND I FEEL THAT WHAT GOD PUT IN MY SOUL IS IN EVERY MAN'S SOUL FOR IF IT WAS NOT SO GOD WOULD NOT HAVE CREATED US. FOR THIS I WOULD LIKE TO KNOW

HOW CAN A MAN TAKE AN IRON PIPE A IRON CHAIN AND CALL HIMSELF A CHRISTIAN.

WHY

SLAVERY

AMERICA?

2005

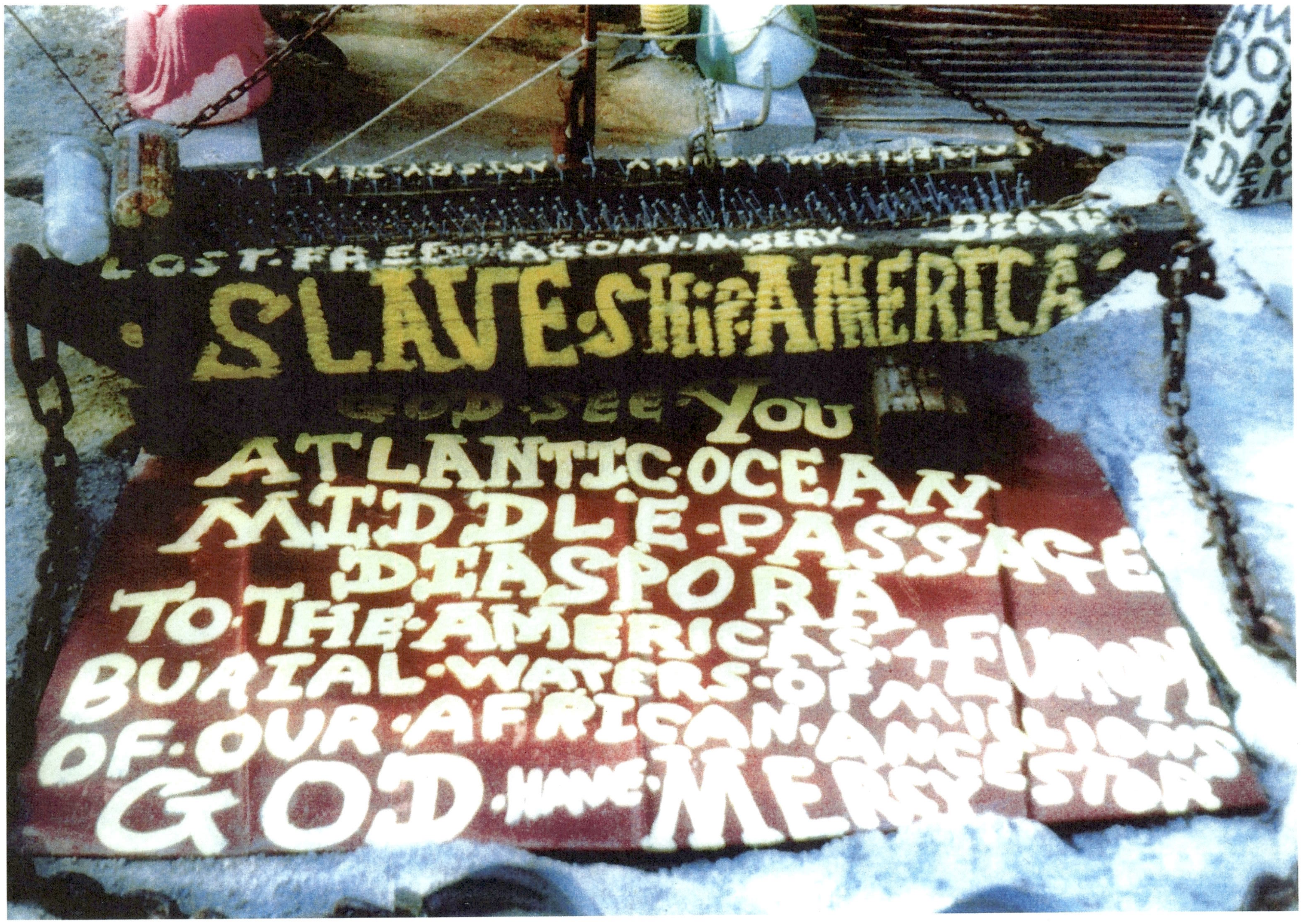
LOST · FREEDOM · AGONY · N · SERY ·   DEATH
· SLAVE · SHip · AMERICA ·
GOD · SEE · YOU
ATLANTIC · OCEAN
MIDDLE · PASSAGE
DIASPORA
TO · THE · AMERICAS · + · EUROPE
BURIAL · WATERS · OF · MILLIONS
OF · OUR · AFRICAN · ANCESTORS
GOD · HAVE · MERSY · STOP

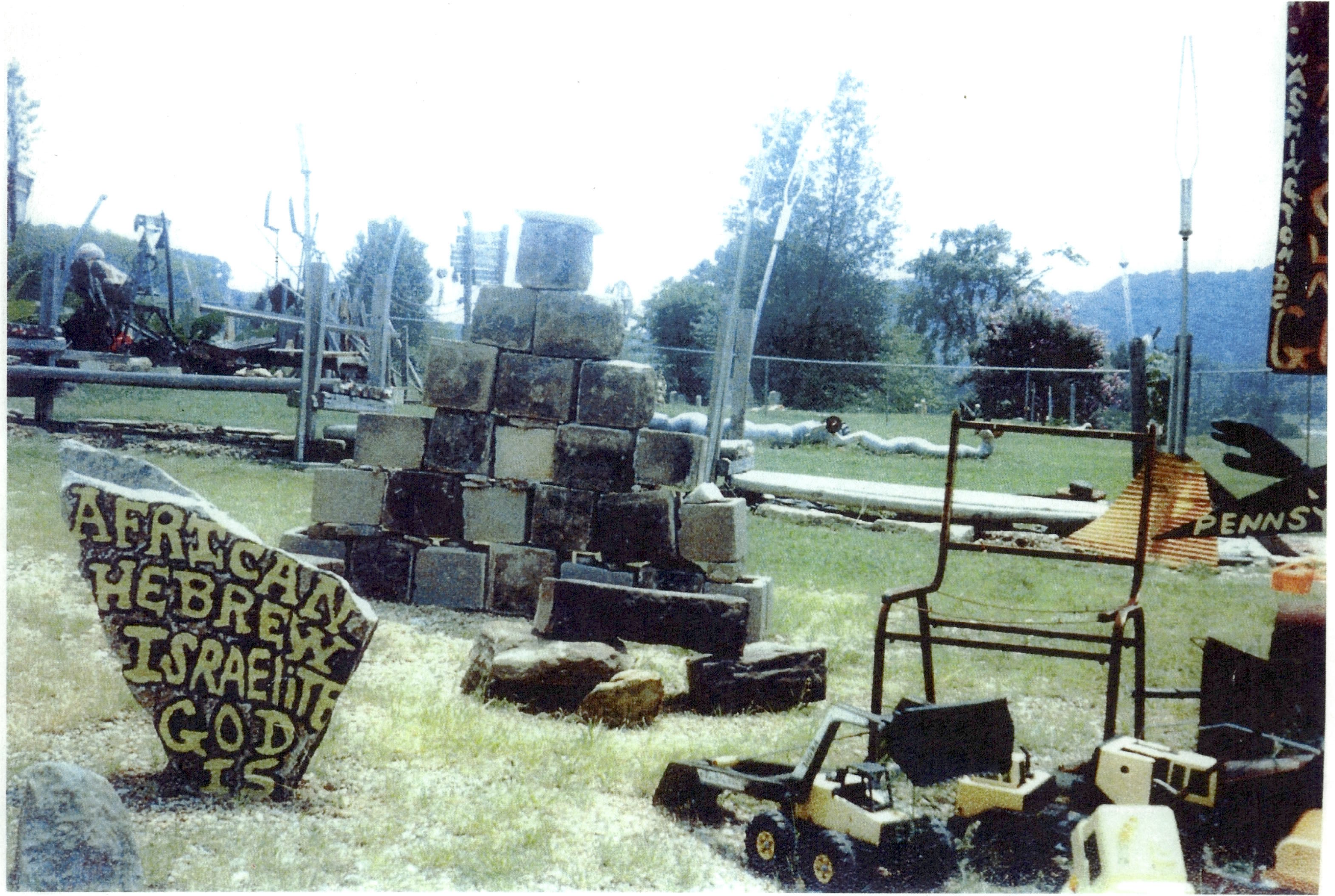
AFRICAN
HEBREW
ISRAELITE
GOD
IS
PENNS
WASHINGTON AC

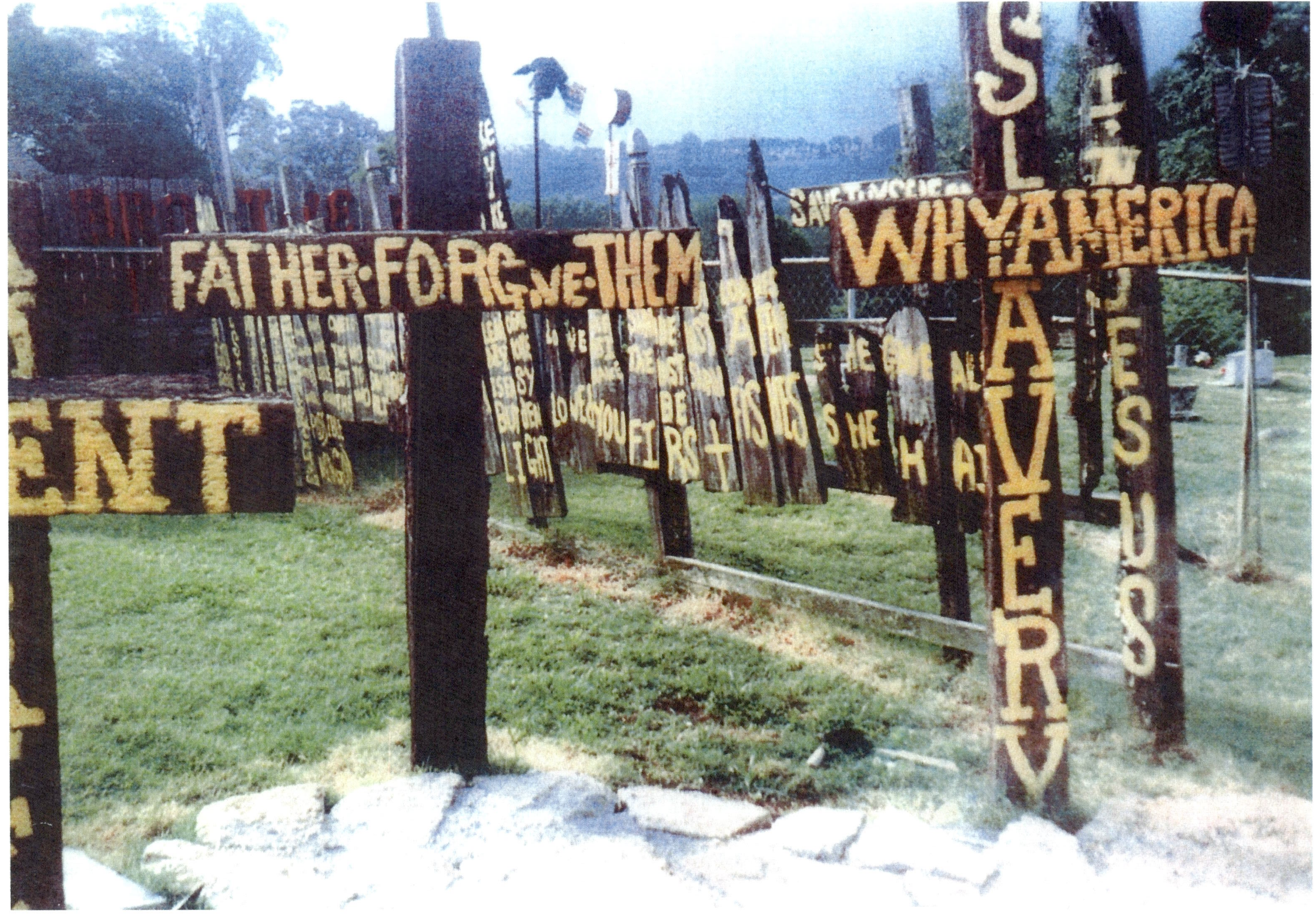

FATHER·FORGIVE·THEM
WHY AMERICA
SLAVERY
JESUS
ENT

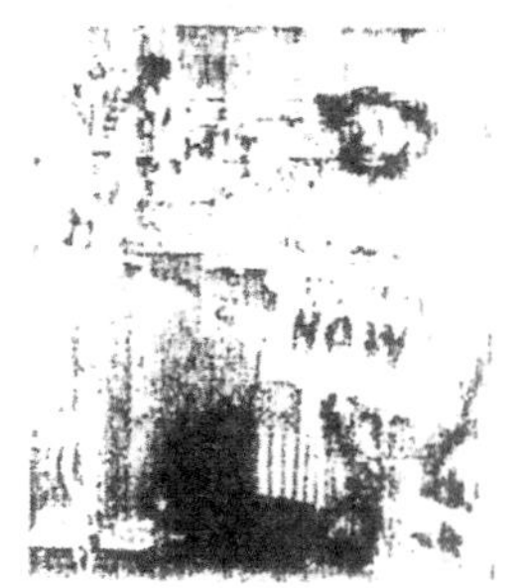

We as a people have a lot to be proud of in our children. For we haven't stride away from them! For we have given them love, trust and a sense of knowing who they are! For we haven't been too proud to kneel on our knees and pray when times get hard! This that we have wasn't given to us on a silver platter We are called troublemakers, agitators, militants, communists, and many other names that have been labeled on us for no reason at all. For we didn't make the trouble! The trouble was made when we as a people was chained and shackled and driven from our motherland like a herd of cattle headed for the slaughter pen. We didn't force ourselves on this country, this country forced itself on us! We have carried our load of the burden of this country for a long time and gotten nothing in return but hate, bigotry, discrimination and injustice. This is 2005 but it might as well be 1805. Still there is much heartache and hurt the black race goes through! When our country calls us to service, we are always there, but when it is all over, the black race is still left in the cold with nowhere to go. How could a free country, born from a democracy, enslave another free human being? This is what happened to the black race! We as a people had our own civilization, our own culture and our own country! This country did not want the black race to even learn to read and write, but we learned and it cost many their lives! A country whose roots consist of the constitution of the law of the land, the Bill of Rights and the many other man-made laws for a free country did not make the black man free!

WE ARE NOT FREE YET!

HE HAS BEEN INSTILLED THE QUALITIES TAUGHT BY JESUS OF LOVE AND KINDNESS.

HOW IS IT THAT WOMEN GOT BEAT DOWN TO THE GROUND EVEN WITH BABIES IN THEIR ARMS. THEY DID THIS TO WHOMEVER STOOD IN THEIR WAY. THEN AFTER THEY WERE KICKED TO THE GROUND THEY WERE THEN SPIT ON OR DRUG OFF AWAY FROM THEIR FAMILIES AND LOVED ONES INTO DUNGEONS FOR THE REST OF THEIR LIVES. THE WHITE MAN HAS FORGOTEN THAT GOD SAID THAT WHICH YOU DO UNTO THE LESS OF US YOU DO UNTO ME. THE BLACK MAN CAN TAKE ALL OF THIS BECAUSE GOD IS IN HIM AND HE WILL NEVER LEAVE HIM.

[PUT ON PAPER 1979, 26 YEARS AGO WHEN THE PLANT SHUT DOWN IN BIRMINGHAM]

IN THE NAME OF JESUS

MAY 11 2005 26 YEARS AFTER THE PLANT SHUT DOWN IN BIRMINGHAM, I BEGAN TO WRITE THE BOOK UNTIL I COMPLETED IT. LORD MY PRAYER IS TO FORGIVE AT THIS TIME AND SAVE US, MY LORD THY GOD LET YOUR CHILDREN THAT HAVE EARS TO HEAR LET THEM HEAR AND ALLOW THEIR EYES TO BE OPENED. AWAKE THEM FROM THEIR SLEEP AND HAVE MERCY ON US AND DELIVERY US AT THIS TIME O LORD. LORD GUIDES MY HAND TO WRITE MY HEART TO BE HUMBLE GIVE ME LOVE AND PEACE. LORD I PRAY THAT YU GIVE ME YOUR WISDOM KNOWLEDGE AND UNDERSTANDING, TO YOU THROUGH ME THE BEGINNING OF A LINK OF A JOURNEY OF 400 YEARS. AFRICAN HEBREW ISRAELITES ON THE WEST COAST OF AFRICA OR THE PEOPLE OF THE MOTHERLAND, WHOSE WAY IS

AFRICAN

HEBREW

ISRAELITE

2000

GOD, LOVE AND PEACE ONE THAT WAS FREE AND AT PEACE WITH GOD WERE UPROOTED BY THE PEOPLE OF THE UNITED STATES OF AMERICA AND EUROPE. BOTH COUNTRIES CLAIMED TO BE COUNTRIES OF CHRISTIANITY. THE UNITED STATES OF AMERICA A DEMOCRACY WITH THE DECLARATION OF INDEPENCE APPROVED ON JULY 4, 1776, THE CONSTITUTION OF THE UNITED STATES OF AMERICA WAS DECLARED IN EFFECT ON MARCH 4, 1789. OVER 100,000.00 AFRICAN UPROOTED A FREE PEOPLE OF GOD THE BIRTH PLACE OF CIVILIZATIONS. THE PLACE WHERE ALL RELIGION AND SCIENCE ORIGINATED. THE MOTHERLAND THE LAND IN THE HOLY BIBLE KNOWN AS EDEN.

COVENANT WITH

ABRAHAM

2005

GENESIS 2

7 AND ON THE SEVENTH DAY GOD
ENDED HIS WORK WHICH HE HAD
MADE; AND HE RESTED ON THE
SEVENTH DAY FROM ALL HIS WORK
WHICH HE HAD MADE.
3 AND GOD BLESSED THE SEVENTH
DAY, AND SANCTIFIED IT: BECAUSE
THAT IN IT HE HAD RESTED FROM ALL
HIS WORK WHICH GOD CREATED AND MADE.
4 THESE ARE THE GENERATIONS
OF THE HEAVENS AND OF THE EARTH
WHEN THEY WERE CREATED IN THE
DAY THAT THE LORD GOD MADE THE
EARTH AND THE HEAVENS,
5 AND EVERY PLANT OF THE FIELD
BEFORE IT WAS IN THE EARTH, AND
EVERY HERB OF THE FIELD BEFORE IT
GREW: FOR THE LORD GOD HAD NOT
CAUSED IT TO RAIN UPON THE EARTH,
AND THERE WAS NOT A MAN TO TILL
THE GROUND.
6 BUT THERE WENT UP MIST FROM
THE EARTH, WATERED THE WHOLE
FACE OF THE GROUND.
7 AND THE LORD GOD FORMED
MAN OF THE DUST OFF THE GROUND.
AND BREATHED INTO HIS NOSTRILS THE
BREATH OF LIFE; AND MAN BECAME A
LIVING SOUL.
8 AND THE LORD GOD PLANTED
 A GARDEN EASTWARD IN EDEN; AND
THERE HE PUT THE MAN WHOM HE
HAD FORMED.
9 AND OUT OF THE GROUND MADE
THE LORD GOD TO GROW EVERY TREE
THAT IS PLEASANT TO THE SIGHT, AND
GOOD FOR FOOD; THE TREE OF LIFE ALSO
IN THE MIDST OF THE GARDEN, AND
THE TREE OF KNOWLEDGE OF GOOD
AND EVIL.
10 AND A RIVER WENT OUT OF EDEN
TO WATER THE GARDEN; AND FROM
THENCE IT PARTED, AN BECAME

INTO FOUR HEADS.
11 THE NAME OF THE FIRST IS PISON:
THAT IS IT WHICH COMPASSETH
THE WHOLE LAND OF HAVILAH
WHERE THERE IS GOLD;
12 AND GOLD OF THAT LAND IS
GOOD: THERE IS BEWDELLIUM AND THE
ONYX STONE.
13 AND THE NAME OF THE SECOND
RIVER IS GIHON THE SAME IS IT THAT
COMPASSETH THE WHOLE LAND OF
ETHIOPIA.
14 AND THE NAME OF THIRD
RIVER IN HIDDEKEL THAT IS IT WHICH
GOETH TOWARD THE EAST OF ASSYRIA.
AND THE FOURTH RIVER IS EUPHRATES.
15 AND THE LORD GOD TOOK THE MAN,
AND PUT HIM INTO THE GARDEN
OF EDEN TO DRESS IT AND TO KEEP IT.
16 MAND THE LORD GOD COMMANDED
THE MAN, SAYING, OF EVERY
TREE OF THE GARDEN THOU MAYEST
FREELY EAT:
17 BUT OF THE TREE OF THE KNOWLEDGE
OF GOOD AND EVIL, THOU SHALT
NOT EAT OF IT: FOR IN THE DAY THAT
THOU EATEST THEREOF THOU SHALT
SURELY DIE.
18 AND THE LORD GOD SAID, IT IS NOT
GOOD THAT THE MAN SHOULD
BE ALONE; I WILL MAKE HIM AND HELP
MEET FOR HIM.

19 AND OUT OF THE GROUND THE
LORD GOD FORMED EVERY BEAST OF
THE FIELD, AND EVERY FOWL OF THE
AIR; AND BROUGHT THEM UNTO ADAM
TO SEE WHAT HE WOULD CALL THEM:
AND WHATSEVER ADAM CALLED
EVERY LIVING CREATURE, THAT WAS
THE NAME THEREOF.
20 AND ADAM GAVE NAMES TO ALL
CATTLE, AND TO THE FOWL OF THE AIR,
AND TO EVERY BEAST O F THE FIELD;
BUT FOR ADAM THERE WAS NOT
FOUND AN HELP MEET FOR HIM.
21 AND THE LORD GOD CAUSED

A DEEP SLEEP TO FALL UPON ADAM,
AND HE SLEPT; AND HE TOOK ONE OF
HIS RIBS, AND CLOSED UPTHE FLESH
INSTEAD THEREOF;
22 AND THE RIB, WHICH THE LORD
GOD HAD TAKEN FROM MAN, MADE
HE A WOMAN, AND BROUGHT
HER UNTO THE MAN.
23 AND ADAM SAID, THIS IS NOW
BONE OF MY BONES, AND FLESH OF
MY FLESH: SHE SHALL BE CALLED
WOMAN, BECAUSE SHE WAS TAKEN
OUT OF MAN.
24 THEREFORE SHALL A MAN LEAVE
HIS FATHER AND HIS MOTHER, AND
SHALL CLEAVE UNTO HIS WIFE AND
THEY SHALL BE ONE FLESH.
25 AND THEY WERE BOTH NAKED,
THE MAN AND HIS WIFE, AND WERE
NOT ASHAMED.

CHAPTER 3

1 NOW THE SERPENT WAS MORE
SUBTLE THAN ANY BEAST OF THE
FIELD WHICH THE LORD GOD HAD
MADE. AND HE SAID UNTO THE
WOMAN, YEA, HATH GOD SAID, YE
SHALL NOT EAT OF EVERY TREE OF
THE GARDEN?
2 AND THE WOMAN SAID UNTO THE
SERPENT, WE MAY EAT OF THE FRUIT
OF THE TREES OF THE GARDEN:
3 BUT OF THE FRUIT OF THE TREE
WHICH IS IN THE MIDST OF THE GARDEN,
GOD HATH SAID, YE SHALL NOT
EAT OF IT, NEITHER SHALL YE TOUCH IT,
LEST YE DIE.

4 AND THE SERPENT SAID UNTO THE
WOMAN, YE SHALL SURELY DIE:
5 FOR GOD DOTH KNOW THAT IN THE
DAY YE EAT THEREOF, THEN YOUR EYES
SHALL BE OPENED, AND YE SHALL
BE AS GODS, KNOWING GOOD AND EVIL.
6 AND WHEN THE WOAMN SAW THAT
THE TREE WAS GOOD FOR FOOD,
AND THAT IT WAS PLEASANT TO THE
EYES, A TREE TO BE DESIRED TO
MAKE ONE WISE, SHE TOOK OF THE
FRUIT THEREOF, AND DID EAT, AND
GAVE ALSO UNTO HER HUSBAND WITH
HER: AND HE DID EAT.
7 AND THE EYES OF THEM BOTH
WERE OPENED, AND THEY KNEW THAT
THEY WERE NAKED; AND THEY SEWED
FIG LEAVES TOGETHER, AND MADE
THEMSELVES APRONS.
8 AND THEY HEARD THE VOICE OF
THE LORD GOD WALKING IN THE
GARDEN IN THE COOL OF THE DAY:
AND ADAM AND HIS WIFE HID
THEMSELVES FROM THE PRESENCE OF
THE LORD GOD AMONST THE TREES
OF THE GARDEN.
9 AND THE LORD GOD CALLED
UNTO ADAM AND SAID UNTO HIM

WHERE ART THOU?
10 AND HE SAID, I HEARD THY
VOICE IN THE GARDEN, AND I WAS
AFRAID, BECAUSE I WAS NAKED; AND
I HID MYSELF.
11 AND HE SAID, WHO TOLD THEE
THAT THOU WAST NAKED? HAST THOU
EATEN OF THE TREE, WHEREOF I
COMMANDED THEE THAT THOU
SHOULDEST NOT EAT?
12 AND THE MAN SAID, THE WOMAN
WHOM THOU GAVEST TO BE
WITH ME, SHE GAVE ME OF THE TREE,
AND I DID EAT.
13 AND THE LORD GOD SAID
UNTO THE WOAMN, WHAT IS THIS
THAT THOU HAST DONE? AND THE
WOMAN SAID, THE SERPENT BEGUILED
ME, AND I DID EAT.
14 AND THE LORD GOD SAID UNTO
THE SERPENT, BECAUSE THOU HAST
DONE THIS, THOU ART CURSED ABOVE
ALL CATTLE, AND ABOVE EVERY BEAST
OF THE FIELD; UPON THY BELLY SHALT
THOU GO, AND DUST SHALT THOU EAT
ALL THE DAYS OF THY LIFE:
15 AND I PUT ENMITY BETWEEN
THEE AND THE WOMAN, AND
BETWEEN THY SEED AND HER SEED;
IT SHALL BRUISE THY HEAD, AND THOU
SHALT BRUISE HIS HEEL.
16 UNTO THE WOAMN HE SIAD, I
WILL GREATLY MULTIPLY THY
SORROW AND THY AND THY
CONCEPTION; IN SORROW
THOU SHALT BRING FORTH CHILDREN;
AND THY DESIRE SHALL BE TO THY
HUSBAND, AND HE SHALL RULE OVER
THEE.
17 AND UNTO ADAM HE SAID BECAUSE
THOU HAST HEARKENED UNTO
THE VOICE OF THY WIFE, AND HAST
EATEN OF THE TREE, OF WHICH I
COMMANDED THEE SAYING, THOU SHALT
NOT EAT OF IT: CURSED IS THE GROUND
FOR THY SAKE; IN SORROW SHALT THOU
EAT OF IT ALL THE DAYS OF THEY LIFE;

18 THORNS ALSO AND THISTLES
SHALL IT BRING FORTH TO THEE; AND
THOU SHALT EAT THE HERB OF THE FIELD;
19 IN THE SWEAT OF THY FACE SHALT
THOU EAT BREAD, TILL THOU RETURN
UNTO THE GROUND; FOR OUT OF IT WAST
THOU TAKEN: FOR DUS THOU ART,
AND UNTO DUST SHALT THOU RETURN.
20 AND ADAM CALLED HIS WIFE'S
NAME EVE; BECAUSE SHE WAS
THE MOTHER OF ALL LIVING.
21 UNTO ADAM ALSO AND TO HIS
WIFE DID THE LORD GOD MAKE
COATS OF SKINS, AND CLOTHED THEM.
22 AND THE LORD GOD SAID,
BEHOLD, THE MAN IS BECOME AS ONE
OF US, TO KNOW GOOD AND EVIL AND
NOW, LEST HE PUT FORTH HIS HAND,
AND TAKE ALSO OF THE TREE OF LIFE,
AND EAT, AND LIVE FOREVER:
23 THEREFORE THE LORD GOD SENT
HIM FORTH FROM THE GARDEN OF
EDEN, TO TILL THE GROUND FROM
WHENCE HE WAS TAKEN.
24 SO HE DROVE OUT THE MAN; AND HE PLACED
AT THE EAST OF THE GARDEN OF
EDEN CHERUBIMS AND A FLAMING SWORD
WHICH TURNED EVERY WAY, TO KEEP THE

WAY OF THE TREE OF LIFE.

CHAPTER 4

PRAISE THE LORD THEY GOD FOR THE WORD.

I PRAY THAT GOD HUMBLES MY HEART IN LOVE GUIDE MY HAND AND USE ME AS AN INSTRUMENT. IN THE SPIRIT OF THE HOLY GHOST. MY BEGINNING GOD GAVE ME THAT WHAT HE GAVE ALL HUMAN BEINGS.

IN GENISIS CHAPTER 2 VERSES 26. AND GOD SAID, LET US MAKE MAN IN OUR IMAGE, AFTER OUR LIKENESS: AND LET THEM HAVE DOMINION OVER THE FISH OF THE SEA, AND OVER THE FOWL OF THE AIR, AND OVER THE CATTLE AND OVER ALL THE EARTH, AND OVER EVERY CREEPING THING THAT CREEPETH UPON THE EARTH.

27 SO GOD CREATED MAN IN HIS OVEN IMAGE, IN THE IMAGE OF GOD CREATED HE HIM; MALE AND FEMALE CREATED HE THEM.

28 AND GOD BLESSED THEM. AND GOD SAID UNTO THEM. BE FRUITFUL, AND MULTIPLY, AND REPLENISH THE EARTH, AND SUBDUE IT: AND HAVE DOMINION OVER THE FISH OF THE SEA, AND OVER THE FOWL OF THE AIR AND OVER EVERY LIVING THING THAT MOVETH UPON THE EARTH. PRAISE THE LORD THY GOD FOR THE WORD.

A CHILD OF GOD JOW WADE MINTER SR. BORN MARCH 28, 1943 BIRMINGHAM, ALABAMA. I ASKED GOD IN 1989 AFTER SEEING AND LIVING

IN A WORLD WHERE THE HUMAN BEINGS ARE USING SO MUCH HATE AGAINST FELLOW HUMAN BEINGS AND WE ALL ARE OF ONE BLOOD IN

THE NAME OF JESUS BROTHERS AND SISTERS. I ASKED GOD IN THE NAME OF JESUS TO GIVE THE DEFINITION OF RACISM THIS IS WHAT HE GAVE ME.

PRAISE THE LORD.

AND YOU ARE NOT GOD

MY BLOOD IS YOUR BLOOD
FOR THE LORD THY GOD MADE ONLY
ONE BLOOD BUT YOU DENY THIS
AND YOU ARE NOT GOD

MY HEART IS YOUR HEART
FOR THE LORD THY GOD MADE ONLY
ONE BUT YOU DENY THIS
AND YOU ARE NOT GOD

MY HEAVEN AND EARTH IS YOUR
HEAVEN AND EARTH FOR THE LORD
THY GOD MADE ONLY ONE
BUT YOU DENY THIS AND YOU ARE NOT GOD

MY DAY AND NIGHT IS YOUR
DAY AND NIGHT FOR THE LORD
THY GOD MADE ONLY ONE
BUT YOU DENY THIS AND YOU ARE NOT GOD

MY CHILDREN ARE YOUR CHILDREN
FOR THE LORD THY GOD MADE ONLY ONE
BUT YOU DENY THIS AND YOU ARE NOT GOD

MY FREEDOM IS YOUR FREEDOM
FOR THE LORD THY GOD MADE ONLY ONE
BUT YOU DENY THIS AND YOU ARE NOT GOD

MY JOY IS YOUR JOY
FOR THE LORD THEY GOD MADE ONLY ONE
BUT YOU DENY THIS AND YOU ARE NOT GOD

MY FAMILY IS YOUR FAMILY
FOR THE LORD THY GOD MADE ONLY ONE
BUT YOU DENY THIS AND YOU ARE NOT GOD

MY HISTORY AND CULTURE IS YOUR
HISTORY AND CULTURE FOR THE LORD
THY GOD MADE ONLY ONE
BUT YOU DENY THIS AND YOU ARE NOT GOD

MY PEACE AND MIND AND SOUL IS YOUR
PEACE OF MIND AND SOUL FOR THE LORD
THY GOD MADE ONLY ONE

BUT YOU DENY THIS AND YOU ARE NOT GOD

MY FUTURE IS YOUR FUTURE
FOR THE LORD THY GOD MADE ONLY ONE
BUT YOU DENY THIS AND YOU ARE NOT GOD

MY COMPASSION IS YOUR COMPASSION
FOR THE LORD THY GOD MADE ONLY ONE
BUT YOU DENY THIS AND YOU ARE NOT GOD

MY HUMAN RIGHTS AND CIVIL RIGHTS
ARE YOUR HUMAN RIGHTS AND CIVIL RIGHTS
FOR THE LORD THY MADE ONLY ONE
BUT YOU DENY THIS AND YOU ARE NOT GOD

MY MANHOOD IS YOUR MANHOOD
THE LORD THY GOD MADE ONLY ONE
BUT DENY THIS AND YOU ARE NOT GOD

IF YOU ARE NOT GOD
WHO ARE YOU
YOU ARE RACISM
YOU WILL NOT WIN
GOD WILL WIN

JOE W. MINTER SR.

My name is Joe Wade Minter Sr. I was born March 28, 1943, in Birmingham, Alabama. I am the eighth child of ten children. My father was Mr. Lawrence Dunbar Minter. He was born April 2, 1893, and he died on November 29, 1959. His place of birth was Selma, Alabama. He was in the 366th Infantry, World War I France. God gave my father the gift of mechanics. He was very skilled at doing this job. After he was discharged from the Army, he could not use his skill in Birmingham because of racism, *Jim Crow* laws, discrimination, segregation, and apartheid. He was forced to take a job as a caretaker in Elmwood Cemetery in Birmingham in order to feed his family. He worked there for thirty years, working outdoors in all types of weather. God was with my father. God has been with all of the African families in America. God will deliver us on time. Thank you, God. My father worked until his death just to make a better way for his each of his ten children.

My mother is Mrs. Rosie McAlpin Minter, born on January 6, 1904. Her place of birth was Greensboro Alabama. Having birthed ten lovely children, she is definitely an angel sent from God. She is one of the sweetest human beings on earth, a mother that gave her children all that God gave her. She gives love from her heart, and love is returned to her form everyone that comes into her presence. That is the African way: God, love, peace. She gave us motherly wit, common sense, and the verse the whole world shall live by: *The Golden Rule*. Of the ten children, there were only 8 surviving children. She gave birth to a set of twins, that later died before I was born. Two more sisters were born after I was, which completes the family of eight-five sisters and three brothers. My mother brought us up with the word of God, her husband, her hands, little food, and some hand- me-down clothes. At times there would not be enough food for the entire family and during those times, she fed us and not herself. God blessed her and her children.

I went to Washington Elementary School four years. Every teacher there was kind to all of the children. They taught us our ABC's, arithmetic, how to read and write, *The Golden Rule*, devotion, and they even loved us as God loved us. They also taught us that we were important human beings. When

I was in the fourth grade (1954), I transferred to Center Street Elementary, where I graduated in 1957. In

the African schools in Birmingham, the books were always hand-me-downs from the white schools.

They would always be in terrible shape. Some of the books had pages missing, or had been marked

through. With all of this, the African teachers still put out a well educated student that knew who they

were and where they were headed. God was with each of us.

My loving wife, Hilda Jo Patrick Minter, was born December 3, 1946, in Lamar,

Alabama. We were united together by God on February 25, 1969. We are blessed by God

to be together for more than thirty years. Thank you, God for giving me a loving, sweet,

strong, hard-working, understanding, and precious African woman, and a devoted Mother

to our two sons. By her being a good woman she made me a good man. When I was

down, she lifted me up. I love her very much. She asks for only a little. If I had the world

to give her and it would make her happy, I would. She has given me a pat on the back and a smile that

has carried me on for thirty years. Money is not everything. God, love, and peace can bring joy to the

world and save it.

THE MOTHER OF

12 TRIBES

2001

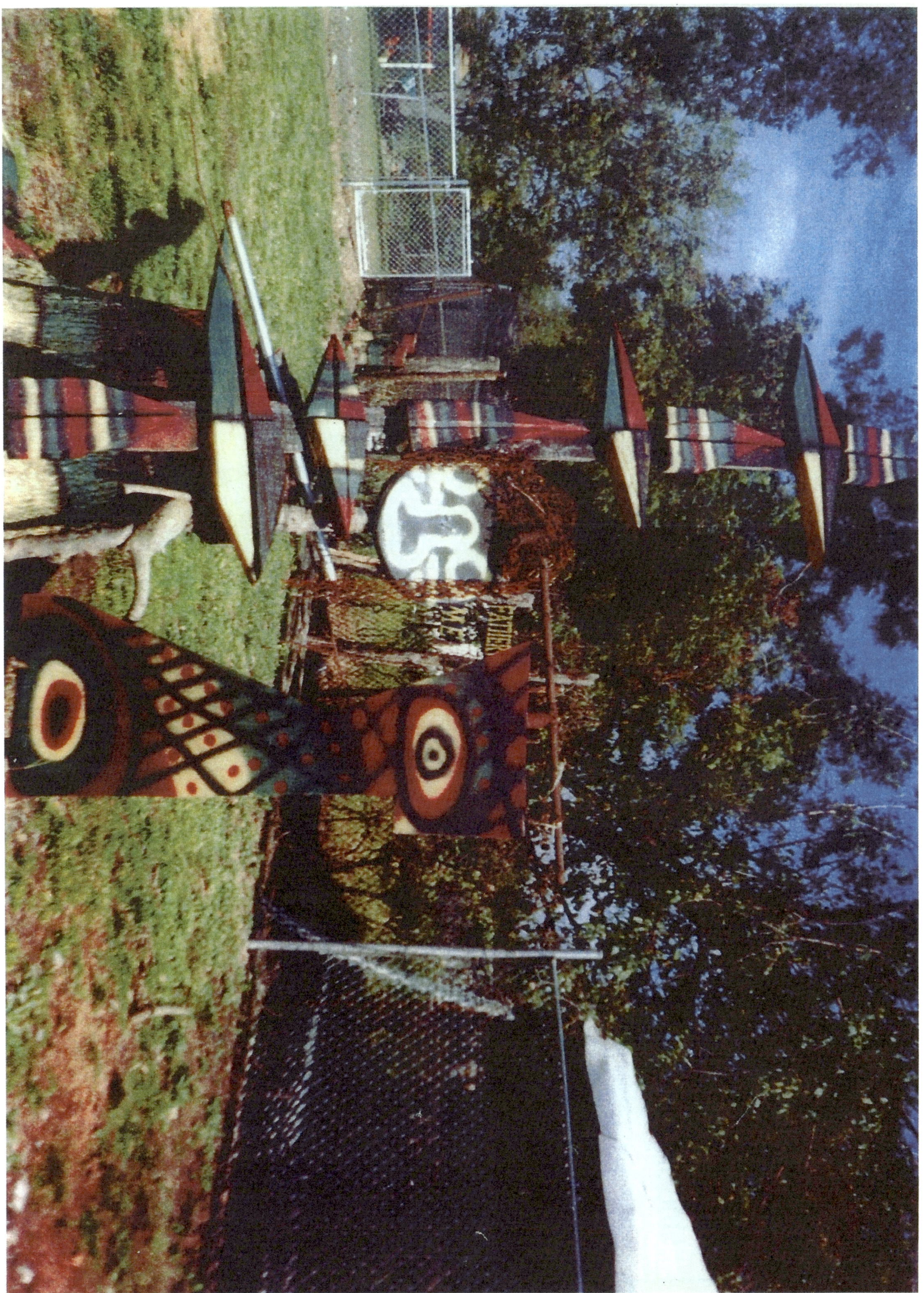

THE AFRICAN PLEDGE

Psychotherapy was practised In Africa by the Egyptians and long pre-dated the Greek, Roman and Hebrew tradition in which much of modern Western psychology is rooted. Imhotep (right), chief minister, astrologer and physician to Djoser (c. 2686-2613 BC), who has been described as "the first figure of a physician to stand out clearly from the mists of antiquity", practised psychotherapy with such skill that he was elevated to the rank of a deity to whom temples were erected at Memphis and on the island of Philae.

Photo © Archives Photographiques, Paris

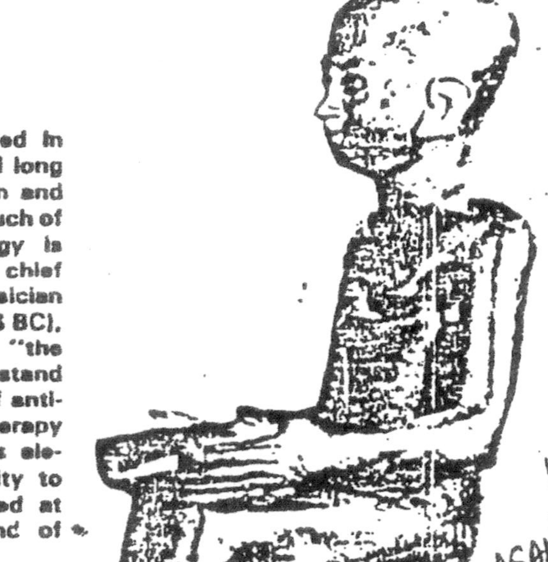

WE WILL REMEMBER THE HUMANITY, GLORY AND
SUFFERINGS OF OUR ANCESTORS,
AND HONOR THE STRUGGLE OF OUR ELDERS;
WE WILL STRIVE TO BRING NEW VALUES, AND
NEW LIFE TO OUR PEOPLE;
WE WILL HAVE PEACE AND HARMONY
AMONG US.
WE WILL BE LOVING, SHARING, AND CREATIVE.
WE WILL WORK, STUDY, AND LISTEN,
SO WE MAY LEARN; LEARN SO WE MAY TEACH.
WE WILL CULTIVATE SELF-RELIANCE.
WE WILL STRUGGLE TO RESURRECT AND UNIFY
OUR HOMELAND;
WE WILL RAISE MANY CHILDREN FOR OUR
NATION;
WE WILL HAVE DISCIPLINE, PATIENCE, DEVOTION,
AND COURAGE;
WE WILL LIVE AS MODELS, TO PROVIDE NEW
DIRECTION FOR OUR PEOPLE:
WE WILL BE FREE AND SELF-DETERMINING;
WE ARE AFRICAN PEOPLE . . . . .
WE WILL WIN!!

HUMAN SUFFERING INDEX

1 LIFE EXPECTANCY
2 DAILY CALORIE SUPPLY
3 CLEAN DRINKING WATER
4 INFANT IMMUNIZATION
5 SECONDARY SCHOOL ENROLLMENT
6 GNP PER CAPITA
7 RATE OF INFLATION
8 COMMUNICATIONS TECHNOLOGY
9 POLITICAL FREEDOM
10 CIVIL RIGHTS
11 TOTAL

The Human Suffering Index was created by the Population Crisis Committee to compare living conditions in 141 countries. Ten measures of well-being are rated from 0 to 10, with 0 as the best rating. Of the 27 countries with extreme human suffering, 20 are found in Africa, with Mozambique having the worst ranking in the world. Of the remaining 7, only Haiti is in the western hemisphere. The United States is rated 5 and Canada is rated 4. Africa's former colonial powers are rated as follows: United Kingdom, 16; France, 7; Portugal, 25; Germany, 6; the Netherlands, 2; and Belgium, 2.

	1	2	3	4	5	6	7	8	9	10	11
ALGERIA	4	0	3	3	9	6	8	9	5	7	54
ANGOLA	10	8	7	10	10	8	10	10	7	6	86
BENIN	10	4	5	7	10	9	0	10	2	5	62
BOTSWANA	7	3	–	5	10	8	6	10	0	2	57
BURKINA FASO	10	6	3	9	10	9	0	10	8	8	73
BURUNDI	10	1	6	4	10	10	5	10	10	9	75
CAMEROON	10	7	6	9	10	7	0	10	8	10	77
CENTRAL AFRICAN REP.	10	6	9	4	10	9	0	10	9	6	77
CHAD	10	8	7	10	10	10	0	10	9	8	82
COMOROS	8	5	7	1	10	9	4	10	4	5	63
CONGO	10	1	6	5	10	8	0	10	7	7	64
EGYPT	8	0	3	4	8	8	5	9	6	8	59
ETHIOPIA	10	7	9	10	10	10	4	10	7	8	85
GAMBIA	10	3	–	4	10	10	5	10	3	3	64
GHANA	9	4	4	9	10	9	9	10	9	8	81
GUINEA	10	6	7	10	10	9	8	10	8	8	86
GUINEA-BISSAU	10	1	8	9	10	10	9	10	7	8	82
CÔTE D'IVOIRE	10	2	–	9	10	8	4	10	9	5	74
KENYA	5	3	7	7	10	9	7	10	9	8	75
LESOTHO	8	2	5	5	10	9	5	10	8	8	70
LIBERIA	9	2	5	10	–	9	6	10	8	9	76
LIBYA	3	0	0	5	–	5	7	6	10	10	51
MADAGASCAR	9	4	7	9	10	10	5	10	6	5	75

	1	2	3	4	5	6	7	8	9	10	11
MALAWI	10	4	4	5	10	10	7	10	10	9	79
MALI	10	4	6	9	10	9	0	10	7	5	70
MAURITANIA	10	4	3	10	10	9	1	10	10	10	77
MAURITIUS	2	0	0	4	9	7	7	7	1	3	40
MOROCCO	5	0	4	5	10	8	3	10	6	8	59
MOZAMBIQUE	10	10	8	10	10	10	10	10	8	7	93
NIGER	10	2	4	10	10	9	0	10	7	8	70
NIGERIA	10	5	5	8	10	10	0	10	6	6	70
RWANDA	10	6	4	4	10	9	6	10	8	9	76
SENEGAL	10	4	5	8	10	8	0	10	5	6	66
SEYCHELLES	2	2	0	4	10	5	0	4	8	9	44
SIERRA LEONE	10	8	6	5	10	10	10	10	8	7	84
SOMALIA	10	5	7	10	10	10	10	10	10	10	92
SOUTH AFRICA	4	1	7	7	9	6	7	5	7	8	67
SUDAN	10	5	6	9	10	9	10	10	10	10	89
SWAZILAND	10	0	5	4	10	8	5	9	8	7	66
TANZANIA	9	3	4	4	10	10	7	10	8	6	71
TOGO	9	5	3	8	10	9	0	10	8	9	71
TUNISIA	4	0	3	2	10	7	3	8	9	7	53
UGANDA	10	4	8	5	10	10	9	10	9	10	85
ZAIRE	10	6	7	10	10	9	10	10	8	8	88
ZAMBIA	9	5	4	5	10	9	10	10	1	5	68
ZIMBABWE	6	3	3	7	10	8	7	9	7	6	66

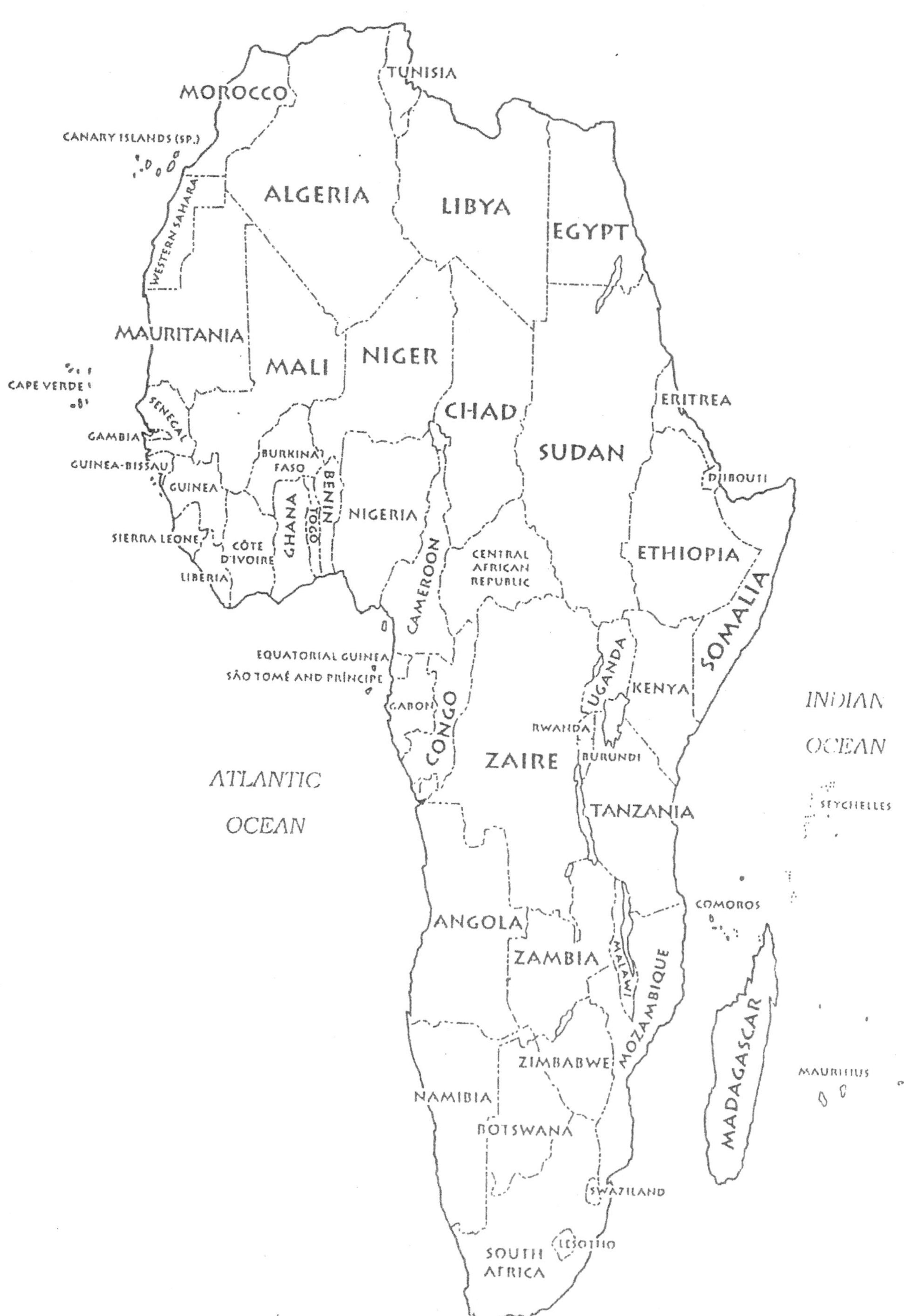

MOROCCO
TUNISIA
CANARY ISLANDS (SP.)
ALGERIA
LIBYA
EGYPT
WESTERN SAHARA
MAURITANIA
MALI
NIGER
CAPE VERDE
CHAD
ERITREA
SENEGAL
SUDAN
GAMBIA
BURKINA FASO
DJIBOUTI
GUINEA-BISSAU
BENIN
GUINEA
GHANA
TOGO
NIGERIA
SIERRA LEONE
CÔTE D'IVOIRE
CENTRAL AFRICAN REPUBLIC
ETHIOPIA
LIBERIA
CAMEROON
SOMALIA
EQUATORIAL GUINEA
SÃO TOMÉ AND PRÍNCIPE
UGANDA
KENYA
INDIAN OCEAN
GABON
CONGO
RWANDA
BURUNDI
ZAIRE
ATLANTIC OCEAN
TANZANIA
SEYCHELLES
COMOROS
ANGOLA
ZAMBIA
MALAWI
MOZAMBIQUE
MADAGASCAR
MAURITIUS
ZIMBABWE
NAMIBIA
BOTSWANA
SWAZILAND
SOUTH AFRICA
LESOTHO

THE NATIONS OF AFRICA

	POPULATION (estimates)	AREA (sq. miles)	CAPITAL	LANGUAGES (official languages in bold)
NORTHERN AFRICA				
ALGERIA	26.000.000	950.000	Algiers	Arabic. French. Berber dialects
BURKINA FASO	9.600.000	106.000	Ouagadougou	French. Mossi. Bobo. other Gourounsi dialects
CHAD	6.000.000	496.000	N'Djamena	French. Arabic. Sara
EGYPT	53.000.000	386.200	Cairo	Arabic. English. French
LIBYA	4.900.000	680.000	Tripoli	Arabic. Berber dialects. English. Italian
MALI	8.800.000	545.190	Bamako	French. Mandingo. Mossi. Bobo. Berber.
MAURITANIA	2.100.000	419.000	Nouakchott	Arabic. French
MOROCCO.W. SAHARA	26.200.000	157.990	Rabat	Arabic. Berber. French. Spanish
NIGER	3.200.000	489.000	Niamey	French. Hausa. Djerma. Buduma. Tuareg
SUDAN	27.700.000	967.000	Khartoum	Arabic. English, Bantu and Nilotic languages
TUNISIA	8.300.000	63.430	Tunis	Arabic. French
COASTAL WEST AFRICA				
BENIN	5.250.000	44.480	Porto Novo	French. Fon. Adja. Yoruba. Bariba
CAPE VERDE	405.000	1.560	Praia	Portuguese. Creole
CÔTE D'IVOIRE	13.500.000	125.000	Yamoussoukro	French. Akan. Dru. Mandinka. Woio
GAMBIA	930.000	4.005	Banjul	English. Malinke. Woio. others
GHANA	16.000.000	92.100	Accra	English, Akan. Mole-Dagbane. Twi. Ga
GUINEA	7.900.000	95.000	Conakry	French. Malinke. Fula. Sussa. 15 dialects
GUINEA-BISSAU	1.300.000	14.000	Bissau	Portuguese. Balante. Malinke. Fulani
LIBERIA	2.600.000	111.370	Monrovia	English. Creole. Kru. Mandingo. Gola
NIGERIA	120.000.000	357.000	Abuja	English. Hausa. Fulani. Yoruba. Edo
SENEGAL	8.000.000	76.000	Dakar	French. Wolof, Peuih. Fulani. Serere
SIERRA LEONE	4.400.000	27.900	Freetown	English. Krio. Mende. Limba. Temne
TOGO	4.000.000	21.990	Lome	French. Kabiye. Ewe. Mina. Cotocoli. Konkomba

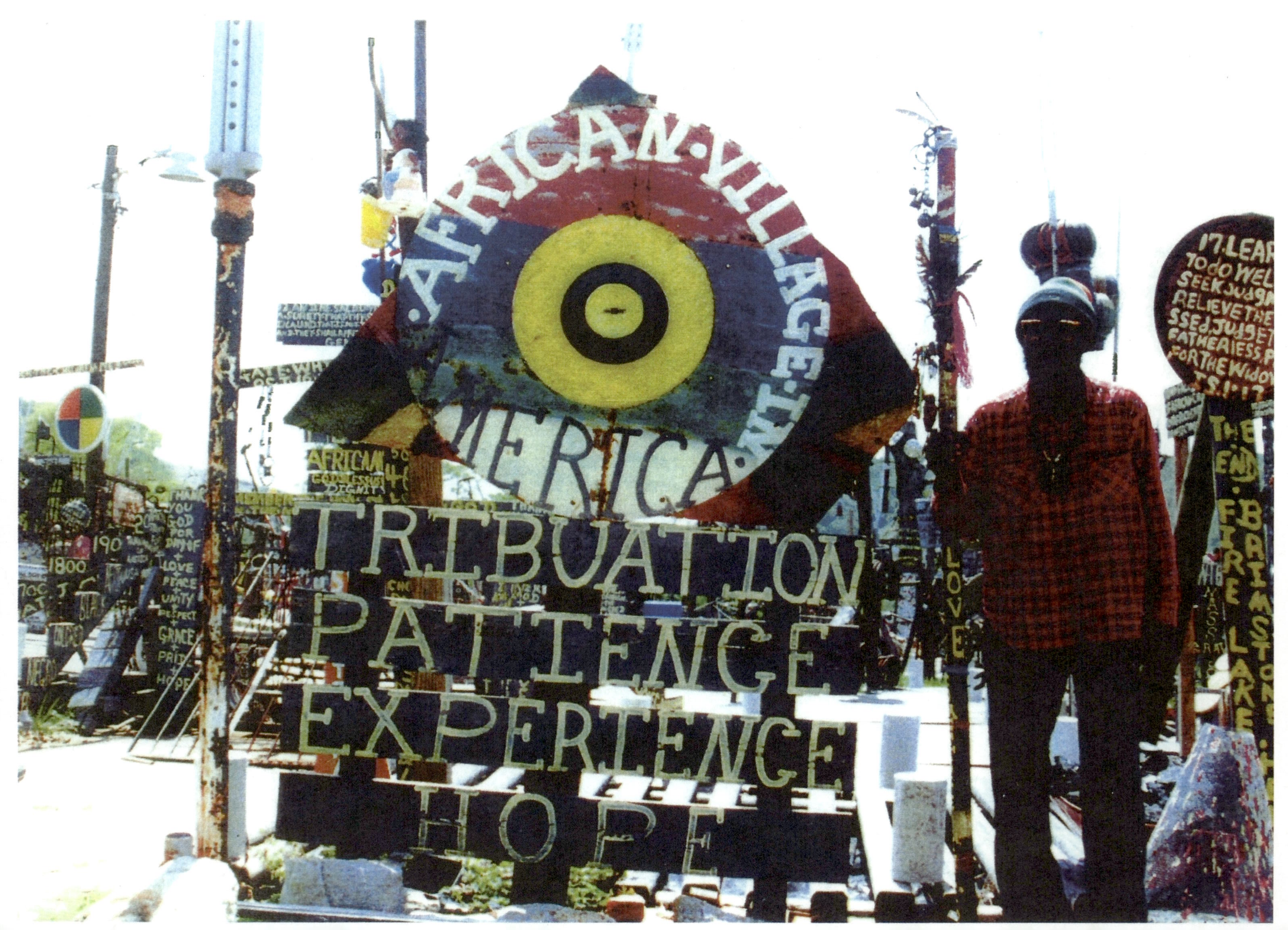
·AFRICAN·VILLAGE·IN·
MERICA·
TRIBUATION
PATIENCE
EXPERIENCE
HOPE
17. LEAR
TO DO WEL
SEEK JUDG
RELIEVE THE
SSED JUDG
FATHERLESS P
FOR THE WIDOW
IS.1:17

I had to learn a lot of jobs over the years. I started off after high school as a dishwasher at a drive-in restaurant, but my job consisted of more than simply washing dishes. I ground the meat up for hamburger patties, cleaned the floor, and whatever else they needed me to do after I finished my job. I worked this job 7 days-a-week, ten hours a day, for 2 years (1961-1963). I left that job to become a "messenger" for University Hospital in Birmingham (now called UAB). We delivered supplies from the warehouse to each department in the hospital. I did extra work in the emergency room on weekends as an orderly. My job was to prep the incoming patients that arrive with wounds and all torn up, and get them ready to see the doctor.

I had to get my driver's license in '63 after I bought a 1953 Plymouth from my brother with the money I had saved up. I had to have a driver's license to go to work in my car. Bull Connor's day. They had this big patrolman, chewing tobacco, and loaded down with pistols, calling me "boy!" He told me to crank the engine, move forward, turn here, there, and after I had driven about three blocks he would say I was speeding and I would be traveling about 20 miles per hour, if that. I did a lot of work to learn everything about the driving test and they still failed me. It was very rough back then.

I was then drafted into the army in 1965. I went through basic training in South Carolina at a "mech and tech" school in Fort Belvoir, Virginia, a six-month course to learn to operate generators. I made if from buck private to Spec4, and operated generators in South Carolina, Missouri, and in Texas. I was discharged in 1967.

Each of my mothers' sons served in the defending of America in the U.S. Army. We have joined a long line of Africans that have put their lives on the line to come back to America and be treated as less than a human being. We as Africans have given America all that we can to give, but there is no love in America for the African. God will have to judge America, for man's heart has hardened in America. May the Lord have mercy on America.

I worked with metal for the next eleven years. I made school furniture, exercise equipment, truck beds, and worked at tearing down old vehicles and rebuilding them into milk trucks. I have also done paint and body work on automobiles. I have been on work crews building roads, and have put up sign boards on the side of the road. I also did about everything regarding construction.

Soon my body began to weaken and my eyes were failing me. I got asbestos dust in my eyes back in the '60s and '70s. I only let them operate on one of them. I have glaucoma and it is incurable. It is as though salt and sand are in my eye all the time. I then had to stop working all together.

In 1979, the company I worked for shut down. I wandered around picking up jobs here and there. Nothing was certain, and I knew I had to regroup, find a way to continue with my life and make the best of it. I saw so much trouble in the world and so many of my people suffering. I was living in a place that looked upon Africans as less than human beings. My ancestors helped build America on the sweat of their backs, in their own blood, in their life, free slave labor, and thy way out was death. I saw how other races were drifting further and further away from one another and how black people were drifting as well. I asked God to help me bring people together as one, for a better understanding even for the smallest child. America had started to lose the family, and when the family is lost, that is the end of all of us here as a people.

I realized that the only way I could preserve this history to hand down to other generations was through art. Art is a universal thing. My idea was to make the art and put a message with it so that it could heal wounds everywhere. I wanted to send the world a message of God's love and his peace for all mankind. I then took on the name "Peacemaker.

When I heard that Birmingham was going to build a Civil Rights Museum, I found my stepping stone. After research however, I found that the main characters were left out of the history. Characters in the freedom struggle (name some here), the foot soldiers. We needed the leaders, but without the foot soldiers, the struggle could not have been won. What happened, then to the recognition for the soldiers? Then I thought about the 400-year journey African Americans have survived.

God gave me the vision of art, to link that 400-year-journey to the Africans in America, link that truth to the children who are turning away from us, and I decided to name what I create *The African Village in America.* It explained the story of the life and struggle we have undergone here in America.

The whole idea handed down to me by God is to use that which has been discarded, just as we as a people have been discarded, and make it visible. All that was invisible, or thrown away, could be made into something everyone could understand. I wanted *The African Village in America* to demonstrate that even what gets thrown away, has a spirit and could survive and continue to grow. A spirit of all the people that have touched and felt that material has remained in that same material. God supplied me with

THE AFRICAN VILLAGE

IN AMERICA

1989

all the materials I needed. I used what other people threw away as junk (what I found on the street, or in flea markets, outlet stores, Goodwill, and even at the Salvation Army). God gave me the message that reflects the art I created for *The African Village in America.*

God, I thank you for the faith and vision, and the dream to be a worker in this vineyard built by your own hands, in love and peace, and to open thy children's eyes.

We as a people of Africa have a story to tell about a 400-year-journey. My ancestors were kidnapped from the motherland of Africa, placed in chains and shackles, uprooted from family and sold into slavery. There were 54,000 shiploads of men, women, and children. 300 of them were packed at the bottom of the ship to sail across the Atlantic Ocean to America. Out of 100 million African people taken into the Western Hemisphere, only 25 million made it alive into the Middle Passage to America. What happened to the other 75 million missing Africans?

God created all men equal. The American Declaration of Independence, passed by Congress July 4, 1776, states that "We hold these truths to be self-evident: that all men are created equal: that they are endowed by their creator with certain unalienable rights; that among these are life, liberty, and the pursuit of happiness." This was a unanimous declaration of the thirteen United States of America by John Hancock. How then was slavery allowed in such a great country as this with such powerful words, and a belief in God? My African ancestors were made to leave their homes and come to the shores of America were kings, queens, tradesmen, skilled craftsmen, artists, and farmers. The Africans had a high culture society and a complex civilization. Our African culture is over 7000-years- old. It all began with the Nubian people of Egypt: Where civilization

BROKEN

PROMISE

1989

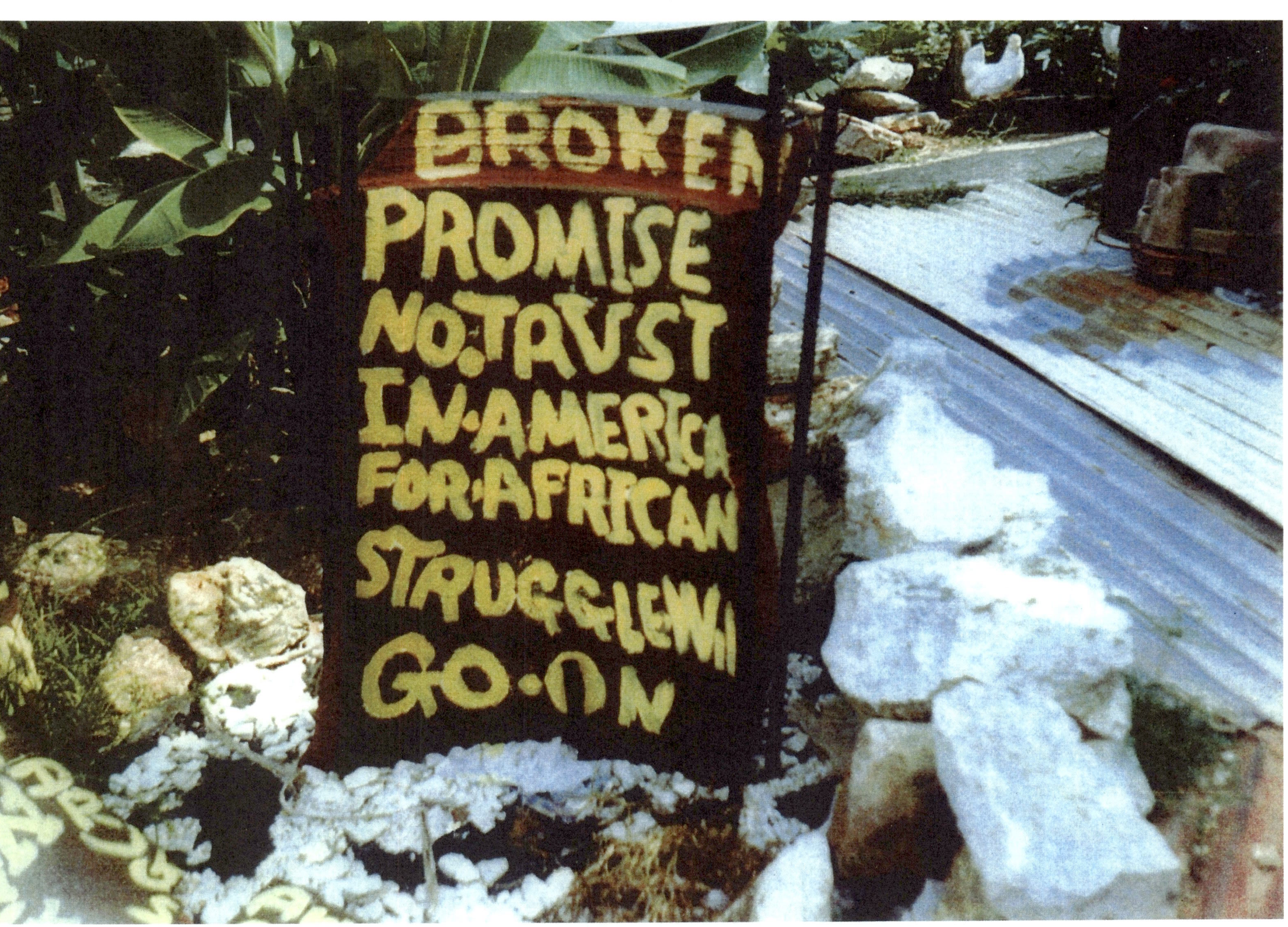
BROKEN
PROMISE
NO.TRUST
IN.AMERICA
FOR.AFRICAN
STRUGGLEWill
GO.ON

Universal Declaration of Human Rights

Whereas recognition of the inherent dignity and of the equal and inalienable rights of all members of the human family is the foundation of freedom, justice and peace in the world,

Whereas disregard and contempt for human rights have resulted in barbarous acts which have outraged the conscience of mankind, and the advent of a world in which human beings shall enjoy freedom of speech and belief and freedom from fear and want has been proclaimed as the highest aspiration of the common people,

Whereas it is essential, if man is not to be compelled to have recourse, as a last resort, to rebellion against tyranny and oppression, that human rights should be protected by the rule of law,

Whereas it is essential to promote the development of friendly relations between nations,

Whereas the peoples of the United Nations have in the Charter reaffirmed their faith in fundamental human rights, in the dignity and worth of the human person and in the equal rights of men and women and have determined to promote social progress and better standards of life in larger freedom,

Whereas Member States have pledged themselves to achieve, in co-operation with the United Nations, the promotion of universal respect for and observance of human rights and fundamental freedoms,

Whereas a common understanding of these rights and freedoms is of the greatest importance for the full realization of this pledge,

Now, therefore, the General Assembly *proclaims* this Universal Declaration of Human Rights as a common standard of achievement for all peoples and all nations, to the end that every individual and every organ of society, keeping this Declaration constantly in mind, shall strive by teaching and education to promote respect for these rights and freedoms and by progressive measures, national and international, to secure their universal and effective recognition and observance, both among the peoples of Member States themselves and among the peoples of territories under their jurisdiction.

Article 1. All human beings are born free and equal in dignity and rights. They are endowed with reason and conscience and should act towards one another in a spirit of brotherhood.

Article 2. Everyone is entitled to all the rights and freedoms set forth in this Declaration, without distinction of any kind, such as race, colour, sex, language, religion, political or other opinion, national or social origin, property, birth or other status.

Furthermore, no distinction shall be made on the basis of the political, jurisdictional or international status of the country or territory to which a person belongs, whether it be independent, trust, non-self-governing or under any other limitation of sovereignty.

Article 3. Everyone has the right to life, liberty and security of person.

Article 4. No one shall be held in slavery or servitude; slavery and the slave trade shall be prohibited in all their forms.

Article 5. No one shall be subjected to torture or to cruel, inhuman or degrading treatment or punishment.

Article 6. Everyone has the right to recognition everywhere as a person before the law.

Article 7. All are equal before the law and are entitled without any discrimination to equal protection of the law. All are entitled to equal protection against any discrimination in violation of this Declaration and against any incitement to such discrimination.

Article 8. Everyone has the right to an effective remedy by the competent national tribunals for acts violating the fundamental rights granted him by the constitution or by law.

Article 9. No one shall be subjected to arbitrary arrest, detention or exile.

Article 10. Everyone is entitled in full equality to a fair and public hearing by an independent and impartial tribunal, in the determination of his rights and obligations and of any criminal charge against him.

Article 11. (1) Everyone charged with a penal offence has the right to be presumed innocent until proved guilty according to law in a public trial at which he has had all the guarantees necessary for his defence.

(2) No one shall be held guilty of any penal offence on account of any act or omission which did not constitute a penal offence, under national or international law, at the time when it was committed. Nor shall a heavier penalty be imposed than the one that was applicable at the time the penal offence was committed.

Article 12. No one shall be subjected to arbitrary interference with his privacy, family, home or correspondence, nor to attacks upon his honour and reputation. Everyone has the right to the protection of the law against such interference or attacks.

Article 13. (1) Everyone has the right to freedom of movement and residence within the borders of each State.

(2) Everyone has the right to leave any country, including his own, and to return to his country.

Article 14. (1) Everyone has the right to seek and to enjoy in other countries asylum from persecution.

(2) This right may not be invoked in the case of prosecutions genuinely arising from non-political crimes or from acts contrary to the purposes and principles of the United Nations.

Article 15. (1) Everyone has the right to a nationality.

(2) No one shall be arbitrarily deprived of his nationality nor denied the right to change his nationality.

Article 16. (1) Men and women of full age, without any limitation due to race, nationality or religion, have the right to marry and to found a family. They are entitled to equal rights as to marriage, during marriage and at its dissolution.

(2) Marriage shall be entered into only with the free and full consent of the intending spouses.

(3) The family is the natural and fundamental group unit of society and is entitled to protection by society and the State.

Article 17. (1) Everyone has the right to own property alone as well as in association with others.

(2) No one shall be arbitrarily deprived of his property.

Article 18. Everyone has the right to freedom of thought, conscience and religion; this right includes freedom to change his religion or belief, and freedom, either alone or in community with others and in public or private, to manifest his religion or belief in teaching, practice, worship and observance.

Article 19. Everyone has the right to freedom of opinion and expression; this right includes freedom to hold opinions without interference and to seek, receive and impart information and ideas through any media and regardless of frontiers.

Article 20. (1) Everyone has the right to freedom of peaceful assembly and association.

(2) No one may be compelled to belong to an association.

Article 21. (1) Everyone has the right to take part in the government of his country, directly or through freely chosen representatives.

(2) Everyone has the right of equal access to public service in his country.

(3) The will of the people shall be the basis of the authority of government; this will shall be expressed in periodic and genuine elections which shall be by universal and equal suffrage and shall be held by secret vote or by equivalent free voting procedures.

Article 22. Everyone, as a member of society, has the right to social security and is entitled to realization, through national effort and international co-operation and in accordance with the organization and resources of each State, of the economic, social and cultural rights indispensible for his dignity and the free development of his personality.

Article 23. (1) Everyone has the right to work, to free choice of employment, to just and favourable conditions of work and to protection against unemployment.

(2) Everyone, without any discrimination, has the right to equal pay for equal work.

(3) Everyone has the right to just and favourable remuneration ensuring for himself and his family an existence worthy of human dignity, and supplemented, if necessary, by other means of social protection.

(4) Everyone has the right to form and to join trade unions for the protection of his interests.

Article 24. Everyone has the right to rest and leisure, including reasonable limitation of working hours and periodic holidays with pay.

Article 25. (1) Everyone has the right to a standard of living adequate for the health and well-being of himself and of his family, including food, clothing, housing and medical care and necessary social services, and the right to security in the event of unemployment, sickness, disability, widowhood, old age or other lack of livelihood in circumstances beyond his control.

(2) Motherhood and childhood are entitled to special care and assistance. All children, whether born in or out of wedlock, shall enjoy the same social protection.

Article 26. (1) Everyone has the right to education. Education shall be free, at least in the elementary and fundamental stages. Elementary education shall be compulsory. Technical and professional education shall be made generally available and higher education shall be equally accessible to all on the basis of merit.

(2) Education shall be directed to the full development of the human personality and to the strengthening of respect for human rights and fundamental freedoms. It shall promote understanding, tolerance and friendship among all nations, racial or religious groups, and shall further the activities of the United Nations for the maintenance of peace.

(3) Parents have a prior right to choose the kind of education that shall be given to their children.

Article 27. (1) Everyone has the right to freely participate in the cultural life of the community, to enjoy the arts and to share in scientific advancement and its benefits.

(2) Everyone has the right to the protection of the moral and material interests resulting from any scientific, literary or artistic production of which he is the author.

Article 28. Everyone is entitled to a social and international order in which the rights and freedoms set forth in this Declaration can be fully realized.

Article 29. (1) Everyone has duties to the community in which alone the free and full development of his personality is possible.

(2) In the exercise of his rights and freedoms, everyone shall be subject only to such limitations as are determined by law solely for the purpose of securing due recognition and respect for the rights and freedoms of others and of meeting the just requirements of morality, public order and the general welfare in a democratic society.

(3) These rights and freedoms may in no case be exercised contrary to the purposes and principles of the United Nations.

Article 30. Nothing in this Declaration may be interpreted as implying for any State, group or person any right to engage in any activity or to perform any act aimed at the destruction of any of the rights and freedoms set forth herein.

Adopted by the United Nations General Assembly, December 10, 1948.

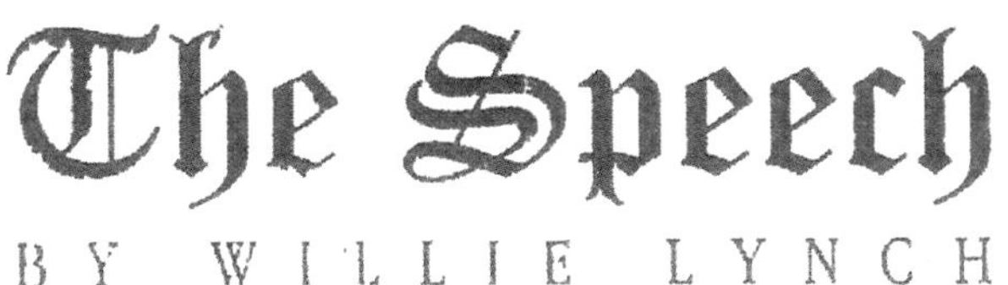

Gentlemen:

I greet you here on the banks of the James River in the year of our Lord, one thousand seven hundred and twelve. First, I shall thank you, the Gentlemen of the Colony of Virginia, for bringing me here. I am here to help you solve your problems with the slaves. Your invitation reached me on my modest plantation in the West Indies where I have experimented with some of the newest and still the oldest methods for control of slaves. Ancient Rome would envy us if my program is implemented. As our boat sailed south on the James River, named for our illustrious King, whose version of the Bible we cherish, I saw enough to know that your problem is not unique. While Rome used cord of wood as crosses for standing human bodies along its old highways in great numbers, you are here using the tree and rope on occasion.

I caught whiff of a dead slave hanging from a tree a couple of miles back. You are not only losing valuable stock by hangings, you are having uprisings, slaves a running away, your crops are sometimes left in the field too long for maximum profit, you suffer occasional fires, your animals are killed. Gentlemen, you know what your problems are; I do not need to elaborate. I am not here to enumerate your problems, I am here to introduce you to a method of solving them.

In my bag here, I have a fool-proof method for controlling your black slaves. I guarantee everyone of you that if installed correctly it will control the slaves for at least 300 years. My method is simple and members of your family or any overseer can use it.

I have outlined a number of differences among the slaves; and I take these differences and make them bigger. I use fear, distrust, and envy for control purposes. These methods have worked on my modest plantation in the West Indies and it will work throughout the South. Take this simple little list of differences, think about them. On top of my list is "age," but it is there only because it starts with an "a;" the second is "color (or shade);" there is intelligence, size, sex, size of plantation, status on plantation, attitude of owner, whether the slaves live on a valley or on a hill, east, west, north, south, have fine hair or coarse hair, or are tall or short. Now that you have a list of differences, I shall give you an outline of action, but before that, I shall assure you that distrust is stronger than trust, and envy is stronger than adulation, respect, or admiration.

The black slave, after receiving this indoctrination, shall carry on and will become self-refueling and self-generating for hundreds of years, maybe thousands.

Don't forget you must pitch the old vs. the young black male and the young vs. the old black male. You must use the dark skinned vs. the light skinned slaves and the light skinned vs. the dark skinned slaves. You must also have your white servants and overseers distrust *all* blacks, but it is necessary they trust and depend on us. They must love, respect, and trust *only* us.

Gentlemen, these kits are your control; use them. Have your wives and children use them; never miss an opportunity. My plan is guaranteed, and the good thing about this plan is that if used intensely for one year, the slaves themselves will remain perpetually distrustful.

Thank you gentlemen

Willie Lynch, 1712

Universal Declaration of Human Rights

Whereas recognition of the inherent dignity and of the equal and inalienable rights of all members of the human family is the foundation of freedom, justice and peace in the world,

Whereas disregard and contempt for human rights have resulted in barbarous acts which have outraged the conscience of mankind, and the advent of a world in which human beings shall enjoy freedom of speech and belief and freedom from fear and want has been proclaimed as the highest aspiration of the common people,

Whereas it is essential, if man is not to be compelled to have recourse, as a last resort, to rebellion against tyranny and oppression, that human rights should be protected by the rule of law,

Whereas it is essential to promote the development of friendly relations between nations,

Whereas the peoples of the United Nations have in the Charter reaffirmed their faith in fundamental human rights, in the dignity and worth of the human person and in the equal rights of men and women and have determined to promote social progress and better standards of life in larger freedom,

Whereas Member States have pledged themselves to achieve, in co-operation with the United Nations, the promotion of universal respect for and observance of human rights and fundamental freedoms,

Whereas a common understanding of these rights and freedoms is of the greatest importance for the full realization of this pledge,

Now, therefore, the General Assembly *proclaims* this Universal Declaration of Human Rights as a common standard of achievement for all peoples and all nations, to the end that every individual and every organ of society, keeping this Declaration constantly in mind, shall strive by teaching and education to promote respect for these rights and freedoms and by progressive measures, national and international, to secure their universal and effective recognition and observance, both among the peoples of Member States themselves and among the peoples of territories under their jurisdiction.

Article 1. All human beings are born free and equal in dignity and rights. They are endowed with reason and conscience and should act towards one another in a spirit of brotherhood.

Article 2. Everyone is entitled to all the rights and freedoms set forth in this Declaration, without distinction of any kind, such as race, colour, sex, language, religion, political or other opinion, national or social origin, property, birth or other status.

Furthermore, no distinction shall be made on the basis of the political, jurisdictional or international status of the country or territory to which a person belongs, whether it be independent, trust, non-selfgoverning or under any other limitation of sovereignty.

Article 3. Everyone has the right to life, liberty and security of person.

Article 4. No one shall be held in slavery or servitude; slavery and the slave trade shall be prohibited in all their forms.

Article 5. No one shall be subjected to torture or to cruel, inhuman or degrading treatment or punishment.

Article 6. Everyone has the right to recognition everywhere as a person before the law.

Article 7. All are equal before the law and are entitled without any discrimination to equal protection of the law. All are entitled to equal protection against any discrimination in violation of this Declaration and against any incitement to such discrimination.

Article 8. Everyone has the right to an effective remedy by the competent national tribunals for acts violating the fundamental rights granted him by the constitution or by law.

Article 9. No one shall be subjected to arbitrary arrest, detention or exile.

Article 10. Everyone is entitled in full equality to a fair and public hearing by an independent and impartial tribunal, in the determination of his rights and obligations and of any criminal charge against him.

Article 11. (1) Everyone charged with a penal offence has the right to be presumed innocent until proved guilty according to law in a public trial at which he has had all the guarantees necessary for his defence.

(2) No one shall be held guilty of any penal offence on account of any act or omission which did not constitute a penal offence, under national or international law, at the time when it was committed. Nor shall a heavier penalty be imposed than the one that was applicable at the time the penal offence was committed.

Article 12. No one shall be subjected to arbitrary interference with his privacy, family, home or correspondence, nor to attacks upon his honour and reputation. Everyone has the right to the protection of the law against such interference or attacks.

Article 13. (1) Everyone has the right to freedom of movement and residence within the borders of each State.

(2) Everyone has the right to leave any country, including his own, and to return to his country.

Article 14. (1) Everyone has the right to seek and to enjoy in other countries asylum from persecution.

(2) This right may not be invoked in the case of prosecutions genuinely arising from non-political crimes or from acts contrary to the purposes and principles of the United Nations.

Article 15. (1) Everyone has the right to a nationality.

(2) No one shall be arbitrarily deprived of his nationality nor denied the right to change his nationality.

Article 16. (1) Men and women of full age, without any limitation due to race, nationality or religion, have the right to marry and to found a family. They are entitled to equal rights as to marriage, during marriage and at its dissolution.

(2) Marriage shall be entered into only with the free and full consent of the intending spouses.

(3) The family is the natural and fundamental group unit of society and is entitled to protection by society and the State.

Article 17. (1) Everyone has the right to own property alone as well as in association with others.

(2) No one shall be arbitrarily deprived of his property.

Article 18. Everyone has the right to freedom of thought, conscience and religion; this right includes freedom to change his religion or belief, and freedom, either alone or in community with others and in public or private, to manifest his religion or belief in teaching, practice, worship and observance.

Article 19. Everyone has the right to freedom of opinion and expression; this right includes freedom to hold opinions without interference and to seek, receive and impart information and ideas through any media and regardless of frontiers.

Article 20. (1) Everyone has the right to freedom of peaceful assembly and association.

(2) No one may be compelled to belong to an association.

Article 21. (1) Everyone has the right to take part in the government of his country, directly or through freely chosen representatives.

(2) Everyone has the right of equal access to public service in his country.

(3) The will of the people shall be the basis of the authority of government; this will shall be expressed in periodic and genuine elections which shall be by universal and equal suffrage and shall be held by secret vote or by equivalent free voting procedures.

Article 22. Everyone, as a member of society, has the right to social security and is entitled to realization, through national effort and international co-operation and in accordance with the organization and resources of each State, of the economic, social and cultural rights indispensible for his dignity and the free development of his personality.

Article 23. (1) Everyone has the right to work, to free choice of employment, to just and favourable conditions of work and to protection against unemployment.

(2) Everyone, without any discrimination, has the right to equal pay for equal work.

(3) Everyone has the right to just and favourable remuneration ensuring for himself and his family an existence worthy of human dignity, and supplemented, if necessary, by other means of social protection.

(4) Everyone has the right to form and to join trade unions for the protection of his interests.

Article 24. Everyone has the right to rest and leisure, including reasonable limitation of working hours and periodic holidays with pay.

Article 25. (1) Everyone has the right to a standard of living adequate for the health and well-being of himself and of his family, including food, clothing, housing and medical care and necessary social services, and the right to security in the event of unemployment, sickness, disability, widowhood, old age or other lack of livelihood in circumstances beyond his control.

(2) Motherhood and childhood are entitled to special care and assistance. All children, whether born in or out of wedlock, shall enjoy the same social protection.

Article 26. (1) Everyone has the right to education. Education shall be free, at least in the elementary and fundamental stages. Elementary education shall be compulsory. Technical and professional education shall be made generally available and higher education shall be equally accessible to all on the basis of merit.

(2) Education shall be directed to the full development of the human personality and to the strengthening of respect for human rights and fundamental freedoms. It shall promote understanding, tolerance and friendship among all nations, racial or religious groups, and shall further the activities of the United Nations for the maintenance of peace.

(3) Parents have a prior right to choose the kind of education that shall be given to their children.

Article 27. (1) Everyone has the right to freely participate in the cultural life of the community, to enjoy the arts and to share in scientific advancement and its benefits.

(2) Everyone has the right to the protection of the moral and material interests resulting from any scientific, literary or artistic production of which he is the author.

Article 28. Everyone is entitled to a social and international order in which the rights and freedoms set forth in this Declaration can be fully realized.

Article 29. (1) Everyone has duties to the community in which alone the free and full development of his personality is possible.

(2) In the exercise of his rights and freedoms, everyone shall be subject only to such limitations as are determined by law solely for the purpose of securing due recognition and respect for the rights and freedoms of others and of meeting the just requirements of morality, public order and the general welfare in a democratic society.

(3) These rights and freedoms may in no case be exercised contrary to the purposes and principles of the United Nations.

Article 30. Nothing in this Declaration may be interpreted as implying for any State, group or person any right to engage in any activity or to perform any act aimed at the destruction of any of the rights and freedoms set forth herein.

Adopted by the United Nations General Assembly, December 10, 1948.

began. Timbucktu of the Kingdom of Mali, with its university and scholars: a city of wisdom. Africa carries 1 to 2000 different dialects and languages. All of this stripped from our African ancestors at the shores of America. They were forced to abide by their laws in chains and shackles. They were naked with only God to protect them and deliver them from the agony, misery, and death. They had to learn the language of their oppressor. They had to learn the culture of the oppressor. In being captured, Africans lost their language, culture, family, our comb for our hair, and our drum for communication. They lost their pride and dignity. Africans became the property of our oppressor, denied human rights for more than 400 years. They were treated like animals: not as Africans, or as human beings, or as brothers or sisters, or even as children of God.

However, we as Africans have survived and will continue to survive in America as African Americans by the will of God and by giving our best work, each one of us. I give my art and the message that stands behind it. Someone else will give labor, the preparation of food, writing, and teaching our little children. God instructs us not to quit, nor to break. To survive is to win, you know. An old oak tree doesn't die, you know. It bends to show its strength. Of each bend that you see, you could look inside of it and see what it went through to carry on. The last got to bend till the end.

We are a beautiful race that cannot be ignored. We have gone through tribulation, but from that experience we learned patience and developed the strength of hope. When you take all of the fruit off a tree, and there is one piece of fruit left, it is the sweetest piece because it has undergone the most to survive. If God chose to bring us along last, we will come last. Something has to come last to be the best.

I look at our book now, the book that tells our story, a story that cannot be buried now, and I understand the role that myself and every other African artists plays. We are like individual drops of water. Everything begins with a drop of water. A river begins with a drop of water. You know how a river do, don't you? When it makes its mind up, ain't nothing going to stop it, don't make no difference what gets put in the way. Once a river starts to flow, it will go all the way down to the sea. Our river is starting to flow now.

PRAISE THE LORD THY GOD.
WE MAY NOT HAVE IT ALL TOGETHER, BUT TOGETHER WE HAVE IT

ALL.

CHAPTER 5

PSALM 23

THE LORD IS MY SHEPHERD; I
SHALL NOT WANT.
2 HE MAKETHE ME TO LIE DOWN IN
GREEN PASTRUES: HE LEADETH ME
BESIDE THE STILL WATERS.
3 HE RESTORETH MY SOUL: HE LEADETH
ME IN THE PATHS OF RIGHTEOUSNESS
FOR HIS NAME SAKE.
4 YEA, THOUGH I WALK THROUGH
THE VALLEY OF THE SHADOW OF DEATH,
I WILL FEAR NO EVIL: FOR THOU ART
WITH ME; THY ROD AND THY STAFF
THEY COMFORT ME.
5 THOU PREPAREST A TABLE BEFORE
ME IN THE PRESENCE OF MINE ENEMIES:
THOU ANOINTEST MY HEAD WITH OIL;
MY CUP RUNNETH OVER.
6 SURELY GOODNESS AND MERCY
SHALL FOLLOW ME ALL THE DAYS OF MY
LIFE: AND I WILL DWELL IN THE HOUSE
OF THE LORD FOREVER.

PSALM 24

THE EARTH IS THE LORDS AND
THE FULLNESS THEREOF; THE WORLD,
AND THEY THAT DWELL THEREIN.
 2 FOR HE HATH FOUNDED IT UPON
THE SEAS, AND ESTABLISHED IT UPON
THE FLOODS.
3 WHO SHALL ASCEND INTO THE HILL
OF THE LORD? OR WHO SHALL STAND
IN HIS HOLY PLACE?
4 HE THAT HATH CLEAN HANDS, AND
A PURE HEART; WHO HATH NOT LIFTED
UP HIS SOUL UNTO VANITY, NOR
SWORN DECEITFULLY.
5 HE SHALL RECEIVE THE BLESSING
FROM THE LORD, AND RIGHTEOUSNESS

FROM THE GOD OF HIS SALVATION.
6 THIS IS THE GENERATION OF THEM
THAT SEEK HIM, THAT SEEK THY FACE,
O JACOB. SELAH.
7 LIFT UP YOU HEADS, O YE GATES;
AND BE YE LIFT UP, YE EVERLASTING
DOORS: AND THE KIND OF GLORY SHALL COME IN.
8 WHO IS THE KING OF GLORY?
THE LORD STRONG AND MIGHTY,
THE LORD MIGHTY IN BATTLE.
9 LIFT UP YOUR HEADS, O YE GATES;
EVEN LIFT THEM UP, YE EVERLASTING
DOORS; AND THE KING OF GLORY SHALL COME IN.
10 WHO IS THIS KING OF GLORY?
THE LORD OF HOSTS, HE IS THE KING
OF GLORY. SELAH.

Isaiah 53

4. Surely he hath borne our griefs and carried our sorrows, yet we did esteem him stricken, smitten of God, and afflicted.
5 But he was wounded for our transgressions, he was bruised for our iniquities: the Chastisement of

our peace was upon him and with his Stripes we are healed.

CHAPTER 6

THE FORERUNNERS OF FREEDOM

Man's gift to the world and humanity, hate, hurt, hunger, homeless, hopeless, heart break, hospitality, homicide, hypocrite, heroin, hydrogen bombs, Holocaust, Hiroshima, Hitler. The African ministers in 63 to follow him his children wanted to be free in America. Reverend Fred Shuttlesworth was called by God to deliver his children out of oppression. Birmingham was chosen by God to soften mans' heart all over the world. The first song of freedom in Birmingham given to us by God was *We Shall Overcome*. Rev. Shuttlesworth put his life on the line to be free. He wanted his people to be free and the whole world to be free as well. Thank you, Jesus.

Rev. Dr. Martin Luther King was called to bring God's blue print of God, love, peace, and freedom for all mankind. He gave him the gift of a clear understood voice that could be heard by all over the world, no matter what the age group was. Rev. Abernathy, Rev. Gardener, Rev. N. H. Smith (fireball), Rev. Phiefer, Rev. Cooper, Rev. A. Wood, Calvin Woods, Rev. Jesse Douglas, Rev. Alford, Rev. Erskine Roulsh, Rev.   , Dr. Carlton Reese, Colonel Johnson, (Buck), Lilly Brown (marching Lilly), "Aint gone Let Nobody Turn me around." James Bevel, J. Armstrong, J. Lay James Orange, C. Price, Lucinda Robey, Tommy Wrenn, Judge V.W. Clemons, Quintin Mitchell Patton, Att. Baker, Vera Brown, Meatball and Sunshine, Poole Funeral Home, A.G. Gaston Motel, African High Schools 1963, Ullman, George C. Bell Parker, Robert C. Johnson, Carver Goodson, Western, Jackson, Hooper City-Hayes, Rosedale, and J. S. Abrams. African College 1963, Miles College, Lawson State Community College, and Daniel Payne.

THE

FORGOTTEN

FOOT

SOLDIER

1990

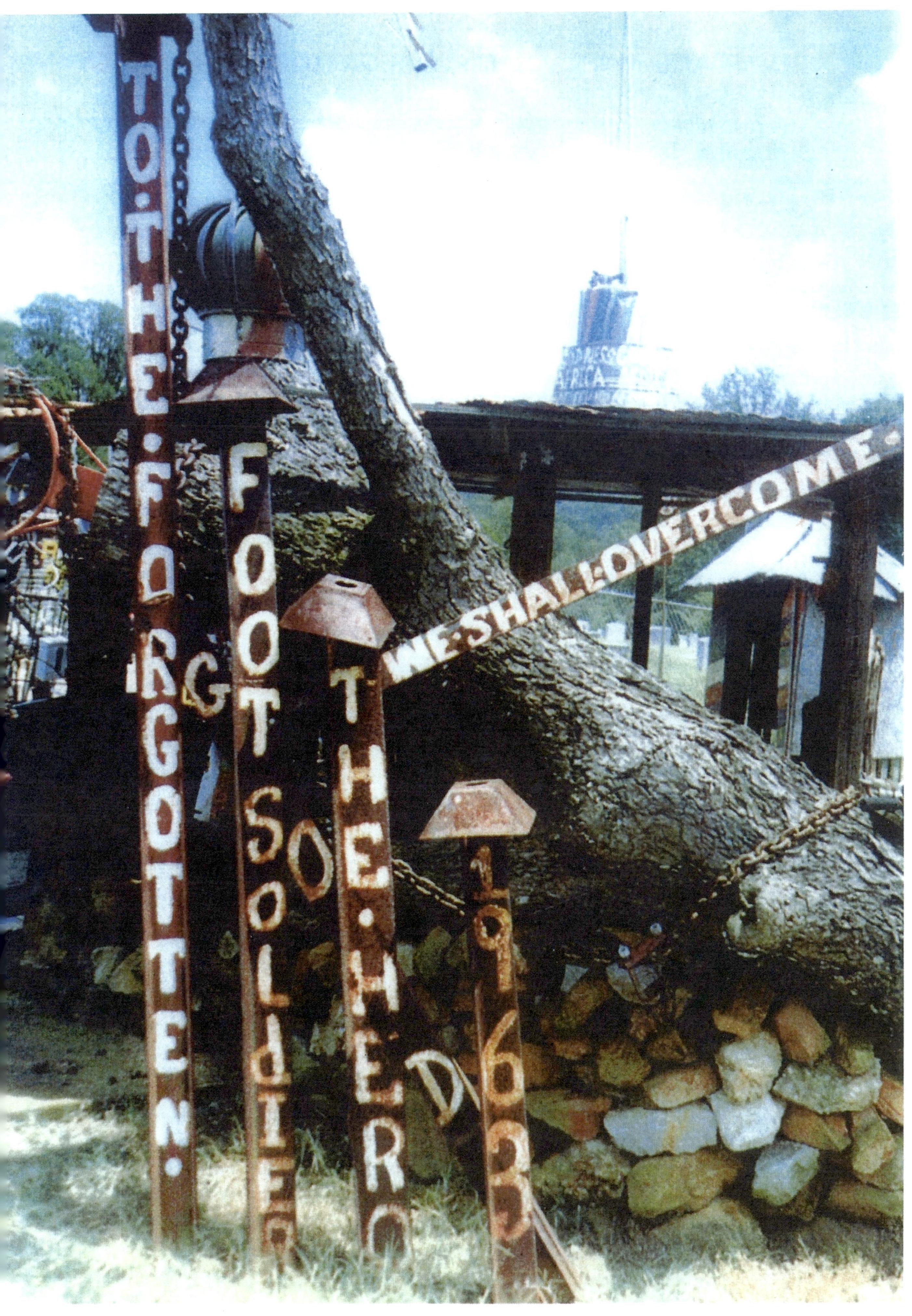

TO·THE·FORGOTTEN·
FOOT·SOLDIER
THE·HERO
1963
WE·SHALL·OVERCOME·

BIRMINGHAM'S RACIAL SEGREGATION ORDINANCES

The following is an excerpt from the original city ordinances for the city of Birmingham. The ordinances are posted in the Institute's Barriers Gallery.

SECTION 369.   SEPARATION OF RACES.

It shall be unlawful to conduct a restaurant or other place for the serving of food in the city, at which white and colored people are served in the same room, unless such white and colored persons are effectually separated by a solid partition extending from the floor upward to a distance of seven feet or higher, and unless a separate entrance from the street is provided for each compartment.

SECTION 597.   NEGROES AND WHITE PERSONS NOT TO PLAY TOGETHER.

It shall be unlawful for a negro and a white person to play together or in company with each other in any game of cards or dice, dominoes or checkers.

Any person, who being the owner, proprietor or keeper or superintendent, of any tavern, inn, restaurant or other public house or public place, or the clerk, servant or employee or such owner, proprietor, keeper or superintendent, knowingly permits a negro and a white person to play together or in company with each other at any game with cards, dice, dominoes or checkers, in his house or on his premises shall, on conviction, be punished as provided in section 4.

ORDINANCE 798-F

An Ordinance To Amend Section 597 Of The General Code Of The City Of Birmingham Of 1944.

Be It Ordained by the Commission of the City of Birmingham that Section 597 of the General Code of the City of Birmingham of 1944 be, and said section is, amended so as to read as follows:

S.E.C. 597 Negroes and White Persons Not To Play Together

It shall be unlawful for a Negro and a white person to play together or in company with each other in any game of cards, dice, dominoes, checkers, baseball, softball, football, basketball or similar games.

Any person, who being the owner, proprietor or

keeper or superintendent of any tavern, inn, restaurant, ballfield, stadium or other public house or public place, or the clerk, servant or employee of such owner, proprietor, keeper, or superintendent, knowingly permits a Negro and a white person to play together or in company with each other, at any game with a baseball, softball, basketball or other ball, in his house or on his premises or in a house or on premises under his charge, supervision or control, shall, on conviction, be punished as provided in Section 4.

Approved Sept. 19, 1950
A true copy,
Eunice S. Hewes, City Clerk
Post-Herald, Sept 21, 1950

SECTION 359. SEPARATION OF RACES.

(a)   It shall be unlawful for any person in charge or control of any room, hall, theatre, picture house, auditorium, yard, court, ballpark, public park, or other indoor or outdoor place, to which both white persons and negroes are admitted, to cause, permit or allow therein or thereon any theatrical performance, picture exhibition, speech, or educational or entertainment program of any kind whatsoever, unless such room, hall, theatre, picture house, auditorium, yard, court, ball park, or other place, has entrances, exits and seating or standing sections set aside for and assigned to the use of white persons, and other entrances, exits and seating or standing sections set aside for and assigned to the use of negroes, unless the entrances, exits and seating or standing sections set aside for and assigned to the use of white persons are distinctly separated from those set aside for and assigned to the use of negroes, by well defined physical barriers, and unless the members of each race are effectively restricted and confined to the sections set aside for and assigned to the use of such race.

(b)   It shall be unlawful for any member of one race to use or occupy any entrance, exit or seating or standing section set aside for and assigned to the use of members of the other race.

SECTION 939. SEPARATION OF RACES.

It shall be unlawful for a negro and a white person to play together or in company with each other at any game of pool or billiards.

Any person, who, being the owner, proprietor or in charge of any poolroom, pooltable, billiard room or billiard table, knowingly permits a negro and a white person to play together or in company with each other at any game of pool or billiards on his premises shall, upon conviction, be punished as provided in section 4.

SECTION 1002. SEPARATION OF RACES.

Every common carrier engaged in operation streetcars in the city for the carriage of passengers shall provide equal but separate accomodations for the white and colored races by providing separate cars or by clearly indicating or designating by physical visible marks the area to be occupied by each race in any streetcar in which the two races are permitted to be carried together and by confining each race to occupancy of the area of such streetcar so set apart for it.

Every common carrier engaged in operating streetcars in the city for the carrying of passengers shall provide for each car used for white and colored passengers, separate entrances and exits to and from such cars in such manner as to prevent intermingling of the white and colored passengers when entering or leaving such car, but this provision for separate entrances and exits shall not apply to the cars operated on the following lines: The South Highlands, Idlewild and Rugby Highland lines or routes.

It shall be unlawful for any such common carrier to operate or cause or allow to be operated, or for any servant, employee or agent of any such common carrier to aid in operating for the carriage of white or colored passengers, any streetcar not equipped as provided in this section. And it shall be unlawful for any person, _ ... ..y to the provisions of this section providing for equal and separate accomodations for the white and colored races on streetcars, to ride or attempt to ride in a car or a division of a car designated for the race to which such person does not belong.

Failure to comply with this section shall be
deemed a misdemeanor.
SECTION 1413.   SEPARATION OF RACES.

Every owner or operator of any jitney, bus or
taxicab in the city shall provide equal but separate
accommodations for the white and colored races by
dividing separate vehicles or by clearly indicating or
designating by visible markers the area to be occupied
by each race in any vehicle in which the two races are
permitted to be carried together and by confining each
race to occupancy of the area of such vehicle so set
apart for it.

It shall be unlawful for any person to operate or
cause or allow to be operated or to aid in operating
for the carriage of white and colored passengers any
vehicle not equipped as provided in this section. And
it shall be unlawful for any person, contrary to the
provisions of this section providing for equal and
separate accommodations for the white and colored
races, to ride or attempt to ride in a vehicle or a
division of a vehicle designated for the race to which
such person does not belong.

Failure to comply with this section shall be
deemed a misdemeanor.

. . . .
. . . .

STATE OF ALABAMA)
                  :
JEFFERSON COUNTY)

I, Eunice S. Hewes, City Clerk of the City of
Birmingham, do hereby certify that the above are true
and correct copies of Sections 369, 597, 859, 939,
1002, 1413 of the 1944 Code of Birmingham.

GIVEN UNDER MY HAND AND CORPORATE SEAL of the
City of Birmingham, this the 25th day of May, 1951.

____
                                       City Clerk

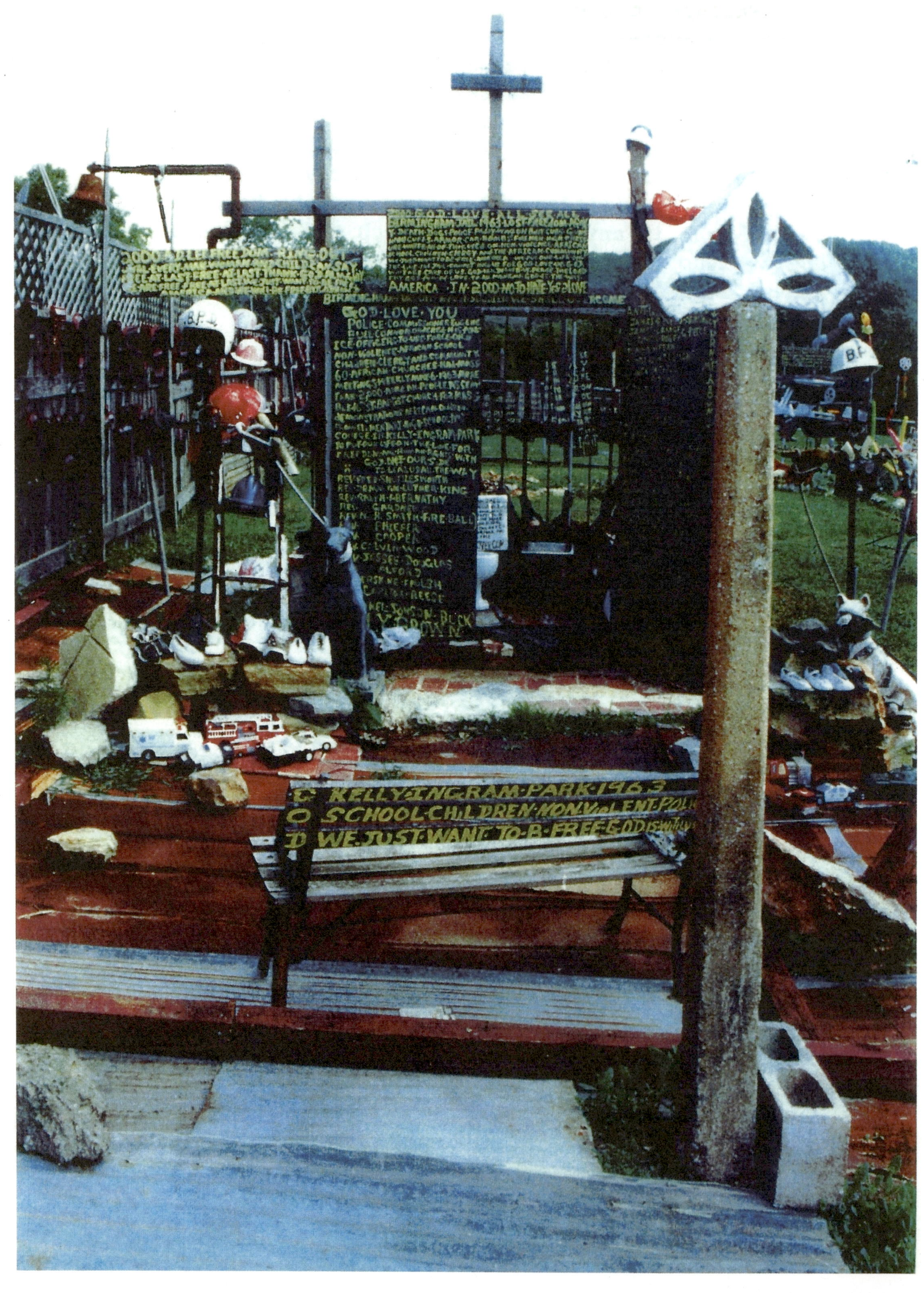

African Radio 1963- Paul Dulley White (tall Paul), Shelly Stewart (Playboy), Rev. Erskine Raulsh, Johnny McLure (Johnny Jive), Willie McKinstry, and Jesse Champion.

Birmingham forgotten historians with all the time of Birmingham preserve in pictures a whole lifetime of work never given a chance to show. What his whole work is about is a good man a God sent man, a good friend, a man in the struggle to free not only himself, but his people as well. He is like me. He has a lifetime story to tell to the world. I have not been given a door to come in and sit down to tell the world my story. The story of a 400-year struggle of him and the African people. I thank God for Odis Barnes Jones, and his brothers; Willie Kelly Jones, David Lee Jones, George Eugene Jones, and Timothy Barnes.

God loves you- Peace to all mankind and the world

CHAPTER 7

IRREVOCABLE FORCE

Police commissioner Eugene (Bull) Connor ordered his police officers to use force on unarmed, non-violent African school children and clergy. In the community African churches had mass meetings weekly. On May 6, 1963, more than 8,000 African people assembled at the 16th street Baptist Church for a mass demonstration. African children from elementary school, high school, and college assembled at Kelly Ingram Park to put their lives on the line for freedom, human rights, and the right to vote with only God on our side to help lead the way. God loves and sees all.

Birmingham Jail 1963

We lost our freedom, agony, death, dogs, police, paddy wagons, Billy clubs, guns, hand cuffs. We were carried off into armored cars, bombed, shot with high pressure water by firemen. All of this force was used against non-violent African school children, the clergy and the African community. We just wanted to be free Americans. We put our lives on the line, but jails could not hold us. God loved us and took care of us. God delivered us. Praise to the Lord thy God. Peace and love to all mankind. God is the way America shall overcome. Dr. Martin Luther King's letter form the Birmingham Jail written on sides of newspaper and toilet paper to all mankind in God, love, peace, and thousands of African School children were put in jail and in criminal cages at fair park for exercising their human rights and to enable them their freedom. March on Washington D.C. 28 Aug. 1963 250, 000 people were present to hear Dr. Martin Luther King Jr. *I Have a Dream* speech. It was a day of repentance, brotherhood and sisterhood, love, peace, prayer, hope, and non-violence. *We Shall Overcome* was heard for miles around. In Selma, Alabama on Edmund Pettus Bridge, "Bloody Sunday" took place on March 7, 1965. God will take care of you. 600 non-violent marchers were attacked by dogs, and state troopers. Their posses' were on horses and they chased, clubbed, kicked and spit on the marchers. They called them names and they had nothing but hate in their hearts for those people. They beat them until they returned to the

African church. Their acts of violence were shown all over the world. There was so much hate for the African brother. All they wanted was their freedom, and have the right to vote and receive their human rights like everyone else.

In 1961, I we lived on the streets of Titusville. Early one morning around 2:00 a.m. in the morning as we slept, the Birmingham police kicked our door in and drug my brother and myself out of the house. My brother was beaten so bad, I could hardly recognize his face. The same police officers wanted to do me in and I told them I was in school and to do whatever they wanted to do, but that we had done nothing. That is how it was while Bull Connor, George Wallace, and the Jim Crow laws were powerful. Those years were the worst years for beating and brutalization or the killing of African men by white police than anytime or anywhere. In Rev. Dr. Martin Luther King Jr. was given the honor of being the noble peace prize winner in 1964. It was given to him by God to teach the world the way of God's love, and peace. He was killed by man. MLK 1929-1968

Our dream has been torn and there is no dream for the African here in America as a person. Africans have given all they have for America. Some have given their own lives. Repent America if you believe in God in 2000 A.D. for we are in the last days for the hand of the Lord is upon us. Forgive us our Lord. Thy God hear my prayer. Have mercy on us for our sins. Amen.

THE

BIRMINGHAM

JAIL

1963

CHAPTER 8

THE DEATH OF THE DREAMS OF THE AFRICAN AMERICAN IN 2003
Birmingham Jail 1963
The Lord heard thy cry from his African children in 1963 in jail asking for human rights, to be human, know justice, be able to vote, have public accommodation, and equal opportunity. On Sunday September 15, 1963, four little African girls were bombed to death while attending Sunday school. Those children bear the cross for America. They have cracked the door just a little to allow the African to come in 2000, the door is being closed in America to the Africans again. God sees all.

AN ATTACK ON

AFFIRMATIIVE

ACTION

2003

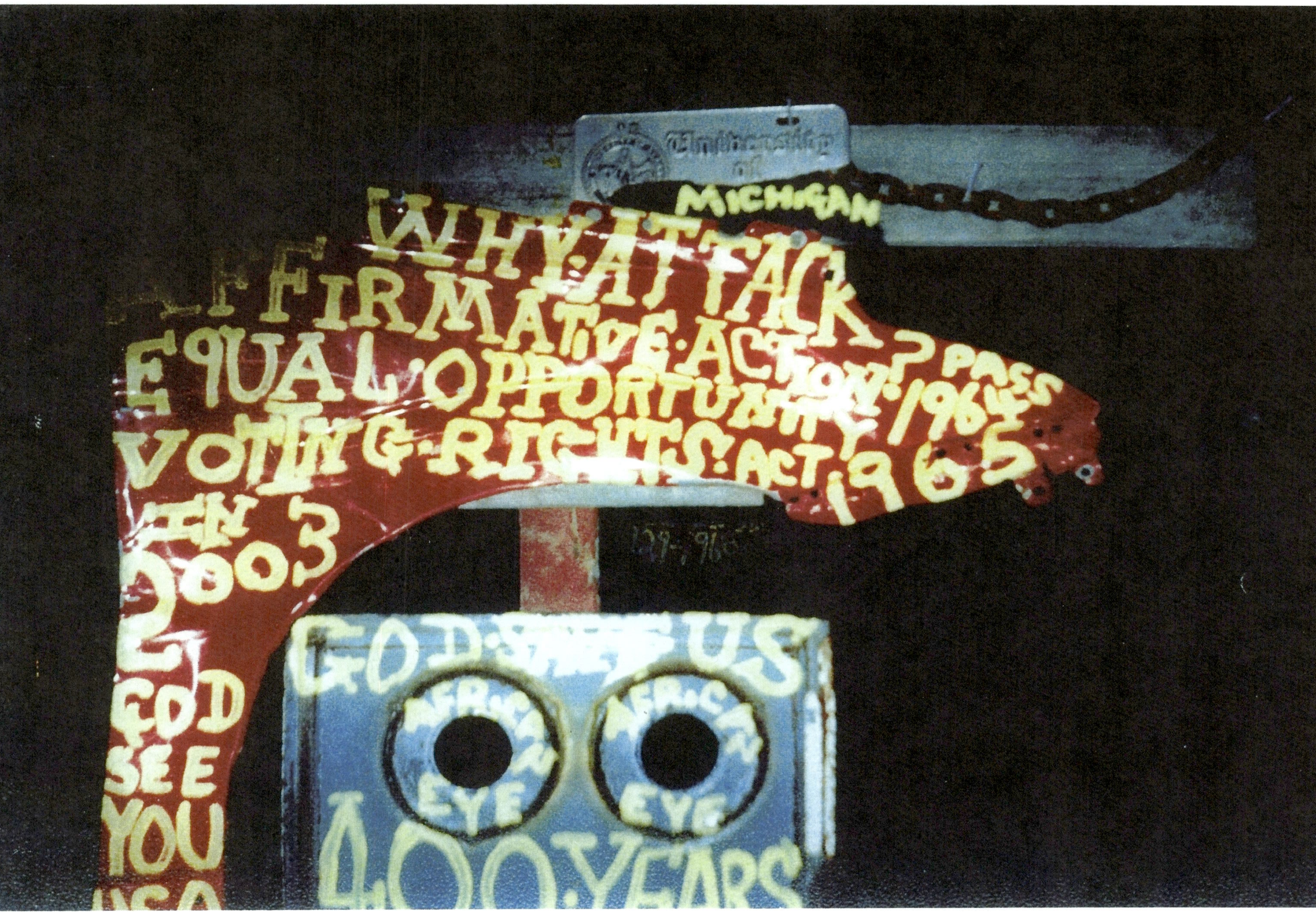
University of MICHIGAN
WHY ATTACK
AFFIRMATIVE ACTION? PASS
EQUAL OPPORTUNITY 1964
VOTING RIGHTS ACT 1965
IN 2003
GOD SEE YOU USA
GOD SEES US
AFRICAN EYE
AFRICAN EYE
400 YEARS

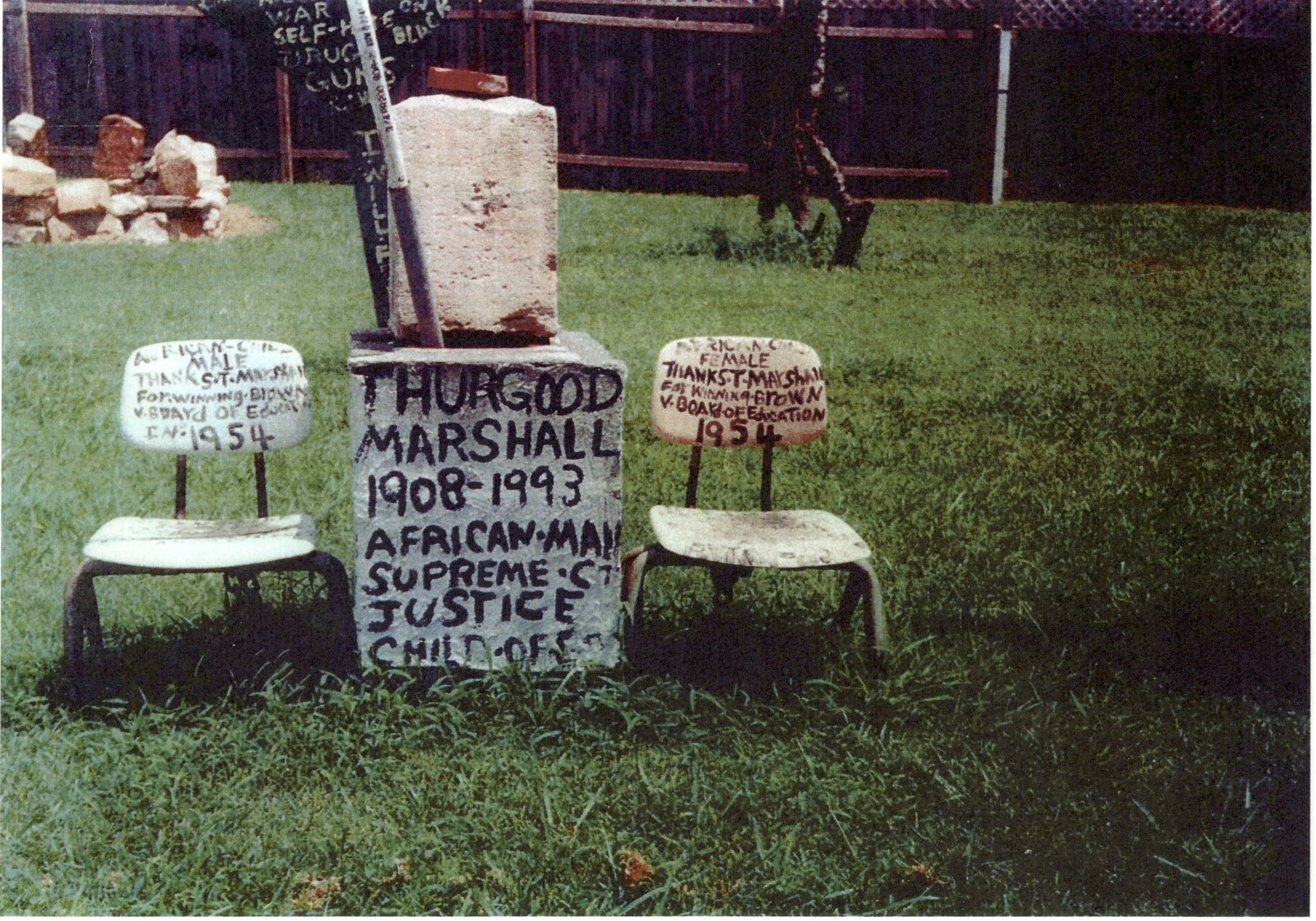
AFRICAN-CHILD
MALE
THANKS.T.MARSHALL
FOR WINNING BROWN
V.BOARD OF EDUCATION
IN 1954
THURGOOD
MARSHALL
1908-1993
AFRICAN-MALE
SUPREME.CT
JUSTICE
CHILD OF
AFRICAN-CHILD
FEMALE
THANKS.T.MARSHALL
FOR WINNING BROWN
V.BOARD OF EDUCATION
1954
WAR
SELF-HATE ON BLACK
THRUGH
GUNS

University of Michigan

Affirmative Action passed in 1964

Equal Opportunity

Voting Rights Act 1965

American needs to humble their heart to the Lord's word.

Jeremiah 22

13 *Woe unto him that buildeth his house by unrighteousness and his chambers by wrong that uses his neighbors device without wages, and giveth him not for his work in the name of Jesus,* repent America.

Genesis 15

13 *And he said unto Abram, know of a surety that thy seed shall be a stranger in a land that is not theirs, and shall serve them; and they shall afflict them four hundred years.*

14 *And also that nation whom they shall serve, will I judge. And afterward shall they come out with great substance.*

2005 A.D.

Come together my beloved African father and mother and save the children and thy family community and world. Unite as one in the name of Jesus in these last days praise the Lord.

Revelation 21

4 *And God shall wipe away all tears from their eyes; and there shall be no more death, neither sorrow, nor crying, neither shall there be any more pain: for the former things are passed away*

Revelation 22

12 And, behold I come quickly and my reward is with me to give every man according as his work shall be.

13 I am Alpha and Omega, the beginning and the end, the first and the last.

Thank you Lord Jesus for all that you have done for these your children we have come thus for in faith for thy hand have shown us mercy and Grace we have endowed this land for 400 years and now it is time for them to repent and come unto you while they have time and ask for forgiveness. Lord save us and comfort with the Holy Ghost these your children. I ask these things in your name in the name of Jesus. Amen

The condition of the African Village in America in 2000 we did not have human rights in America. After 400 years of the African struggle and after Thurgood Marshall struggled in the Supreme Court and with the Civil Rights Act of 1964-1965, someone has forgotten the struggle. We have passed on the blood of the 4 little girls who passed away in Sunday school at the 16th st Baptist Church in Birmingham in the 1963 bombing. The African struggle was allowed to sleep for 400 years and we turn on ourselves with self hate instead of self-determination with God to lead and guide us into 2000. Our downfall is destruction, distrust, and division of the African Church in America. Upon this rock, come back to the rock in truth, in unity, and in the name of Jesus. He is coming back soon for the rock and believers in Him and in love, in peace, and in joy. Peace to you.

CHAPTER 9

A RECURRING WAKE-UP CALL

Here are the names of the streets in the African neighborhood: self-hate street, gun street USA, crack street USA, gang warfare street USA, drive-by shooting street USA, babies are killing babies street USA, babies are having babies street USA, self genocide USA. We must lay down the guns and come to Jesus now and do not turn from God. We have no unity and we have even turned away from our children. Break down of the African family in America has caused us to disrespect our ancestors, our elders, ourselves, our family, our mothers, our fathers, our grandmothers, our grandfathers, our sisters, our brothers, and even our God. May the Lord have mercy on us, his children; Africans need to stop the drive by shootings, killings, robberies, sales of crack or any other drugs, and prostitution. Pastors, politicians, and the US government are caught in the crossfire. Innocent African community in USA like men, women, children, babies at home, church, at work, and at school can be killed anywhere. Our gang warfare has gotten out of hand. Man's heart has hardened. Help us God

Solution

We must first turn to God, and say no more gang warfare, no killings, and end the violence. We must put God first for he is the Alpha and the Omega. He created all for form good to do his work he holds all of his creation in his hands as a part of God's creation. The African family way is God, love, and peace. As Africans we can clean up the bad works that we have allowed to overtake us and become a family again. Our Lord, thy God will welcome us with Holy arms. Our self determination is in our hands. Stop all gang warfare, guns, drive-by shootings, killings, and stop the babies having babies, shut down the crack selling and the crack houses, stop the robbings, and prostitution. Come in to the love of God in Unity. He will give you his whole kingdom. Praise God. The Earth is the Lords and the fullness thereof. Save our children. Birmingham why? Jasmine Moore (January 19, 1995- January 29, 1999) was one of our little African girls, also a gift from God for us to love, protect, and teach in the way of God was killed, why? Look at

THE HAND
OF
GOD
FROM
GENESIS
TO
REVELATION
2005

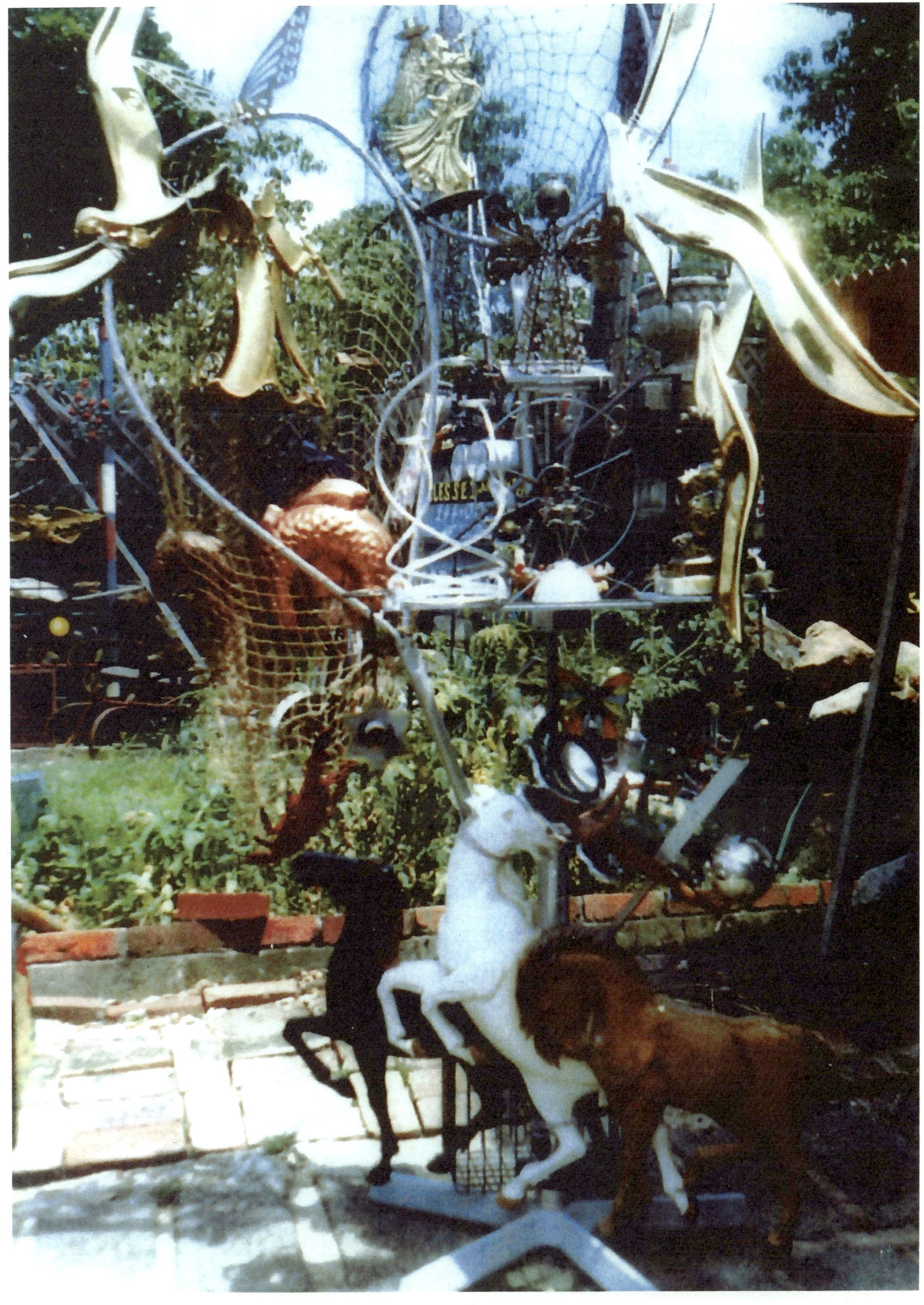

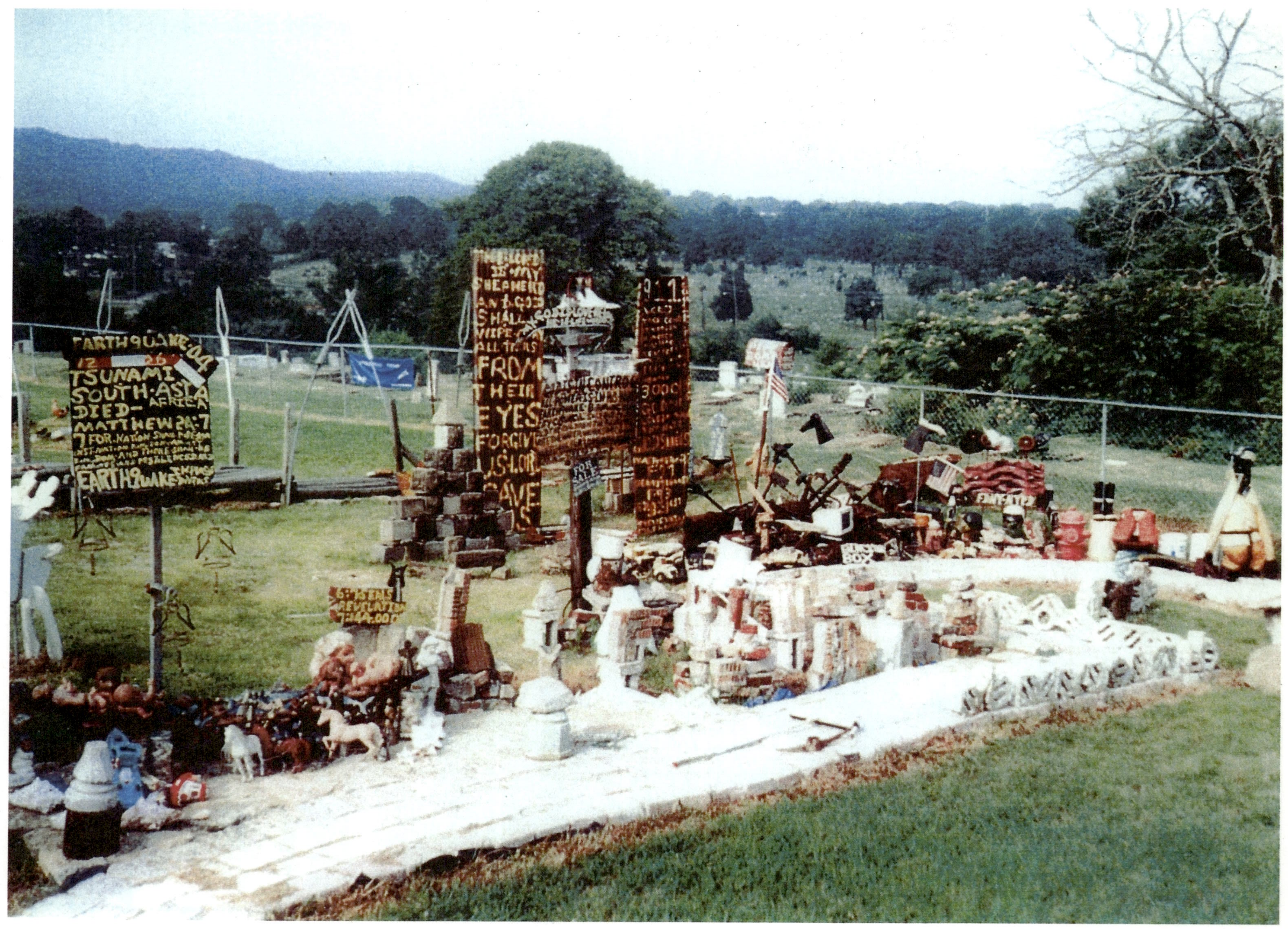
EARTHQUAKE '04
12   26
TSUNAMI
SOUTH ASIA
DIED- AFRICA
MATTHEW 24:7
7 FOR NATION SHALL RISE
EARTHQUAKE
THE LORD IS MY SHEPHERD AND GOD SHALL WIPE ALL TEARS FROM THEIR EYES FORGIVE US LORD SAVE US
911
REVELATION
FOR SALE

the conditions of our communities and schools in 2004. In the name of Jesus show me and my disabled sisters and brothers some love. Save us. Why? Right here in America Benjamin Gruggs was killed by Birmingham police with 24 shots fired into his body. God help us. Stop the killings 3 police officers were killed in the line of duty on June 17, 2004, (in memory of Carlos Owen 58, Charles Bennett 33, Harley Chisholm 41) they are gone but not forgotten. Service and protect African community Thanks Birmingham police, Fire and Rescue, Public Works Street and Sanitation departments, and the postal service. May God bless all of you from the bottom of my heart, thank you very, very much. I can do all things through Christ which strengthens me. Racism, genocide-you are your brothers keeper. I love God, I love myself, I love my family, I love you, and I love peace. I am the way, the truth, and the life. My God is love. He loves all and he is life. 251,000 voters were denied the right to vote in Birmingham, Alabama by spraying fire hoses, and by fire. Why? The African voter's in Birmingham wanted to operate its own water works. It was stolen and taken away from us. We were not allowed to vote on it through petition. Lots of people worked in all types of weather conditions to get 27,000 signatures and it was denied by judge Smallwood. The judge of the probate allowed all of the petition.

God is in control, of all power is in his hands, earthquake, Birmingham city council, sale out of the old the children the right to vote, the water works , the community, and school for love of money making Birmingham a dump 911 2001, F-11, F-175, F-77, and F-93, New York, Washington D.C. Pennsylvania world trade center, Pentagon, hijacked airplanes. Death of police, and fireman in New York. The death toll was almost 3000 people. FDNY lost 343 firemen. God placed love in man and not hate. God Save us. African community elders and children in warzone stand up African warrior lets have God love and peace. God I pray for the African brother and sister to humble their hearts and stop the self-hate and self-genocide for the guns have been turned on our little African girls by the African males who are her protectors. She is the mother of our future. Because we know not of Gods love or peace. No respect without this in your heart and in the way you treat all human beings. All life will come to an end on earth. Thou shall not kill. God forgives us. Save us, come together or we will perish.

On Wednesday April 8, 1998, around 8 p.m.; came a tornado (F-5) to 3 Co. Jeff. Tuscaloosa St. Clair. 300 mph. Winds were 22 miles long, and was on the ground 30 minutes. The Lord had mercy on us. Only 32 died and 221 people were injured. God forgive us for our hate thy will be done. Hate kills and love heals. I met an African brother while I was picking up some stones that had been thrown away on 8th avenue north. He was sent by God. We walked for many hours in the name of Jesus. We both shared the stories of our lives. We were both full of the Holy Ghost. Thanking and praising the Lord. He told me that God put it on his heart to tell me to write a book in 1979 when the (what plant) plant was about to close down. The name of the book was To you through me said my wife. God told her that could be the title for the beginning of the title so I added to the name of the book. The full name for the book that God gave me was: **TO YOU THROUGH ME THE BEGINNING OF A LINK OF A JOURNEY OF 400 YEARS**. I put the pen down in 1979 after I met this African brother who gave me 40.00 dollars and told me to accept it in the name of Jesus. I did accept it. My dear mother passed in 2003 and she was 100 years young. I thank God for her and I know she is looking down on me from heaven. Praise the Lord. She told me that anything someone

THE 911

ATTACKS

2001

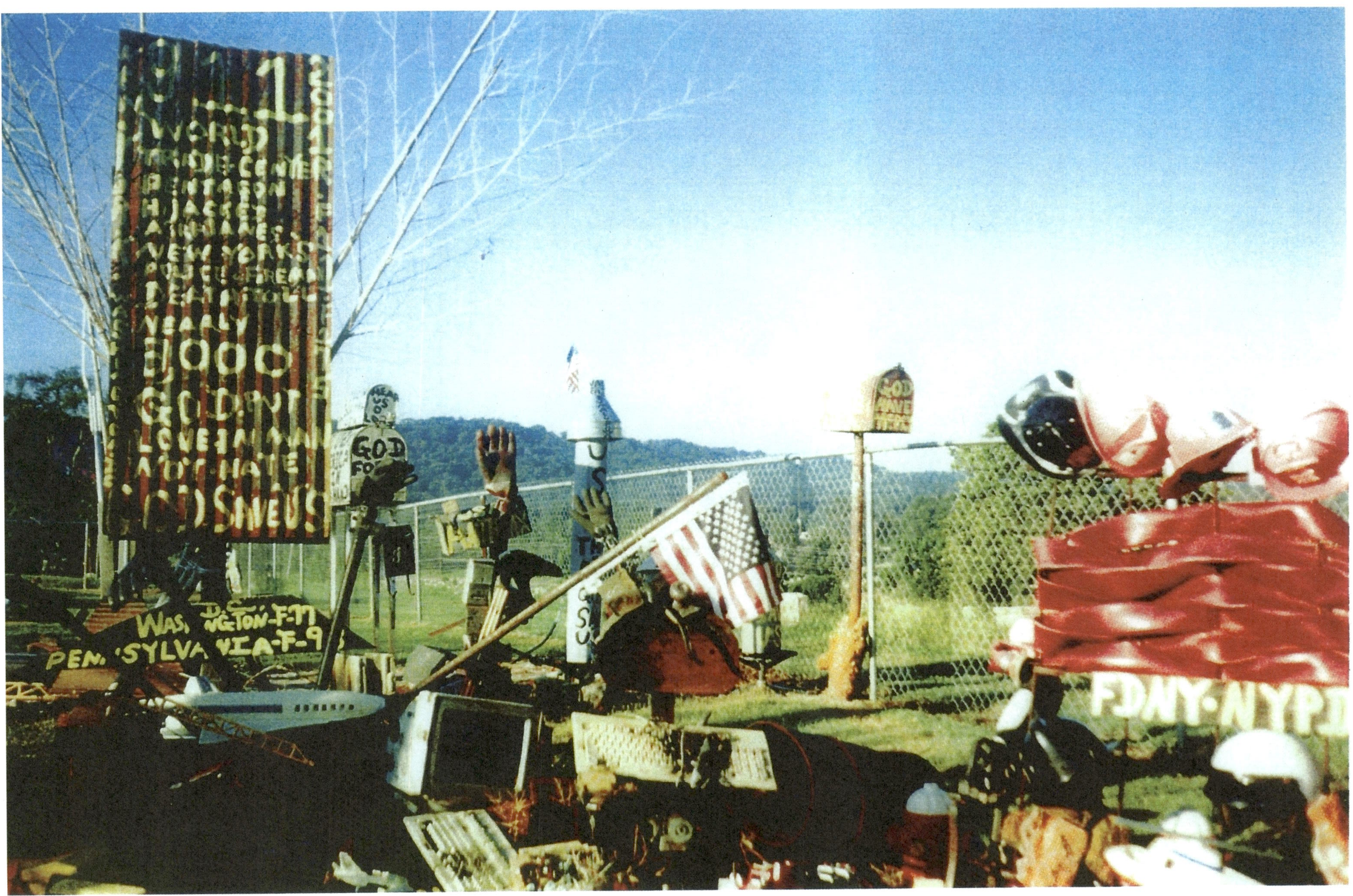

WORLD TRADE CENTER PENTAGON HIJACKED PLANES NEW YORK'S POLICE & FIRE DEATH TOLL NEARLY 3000 GOD DIDN'T LOVE AMERICA HE AT HATE GOD SAVE US
GOD FO
GOD POWER
USA
WAS.NGTON-F-77
PEN'SYLVA.VIA-F-9
FDNY·NYPD

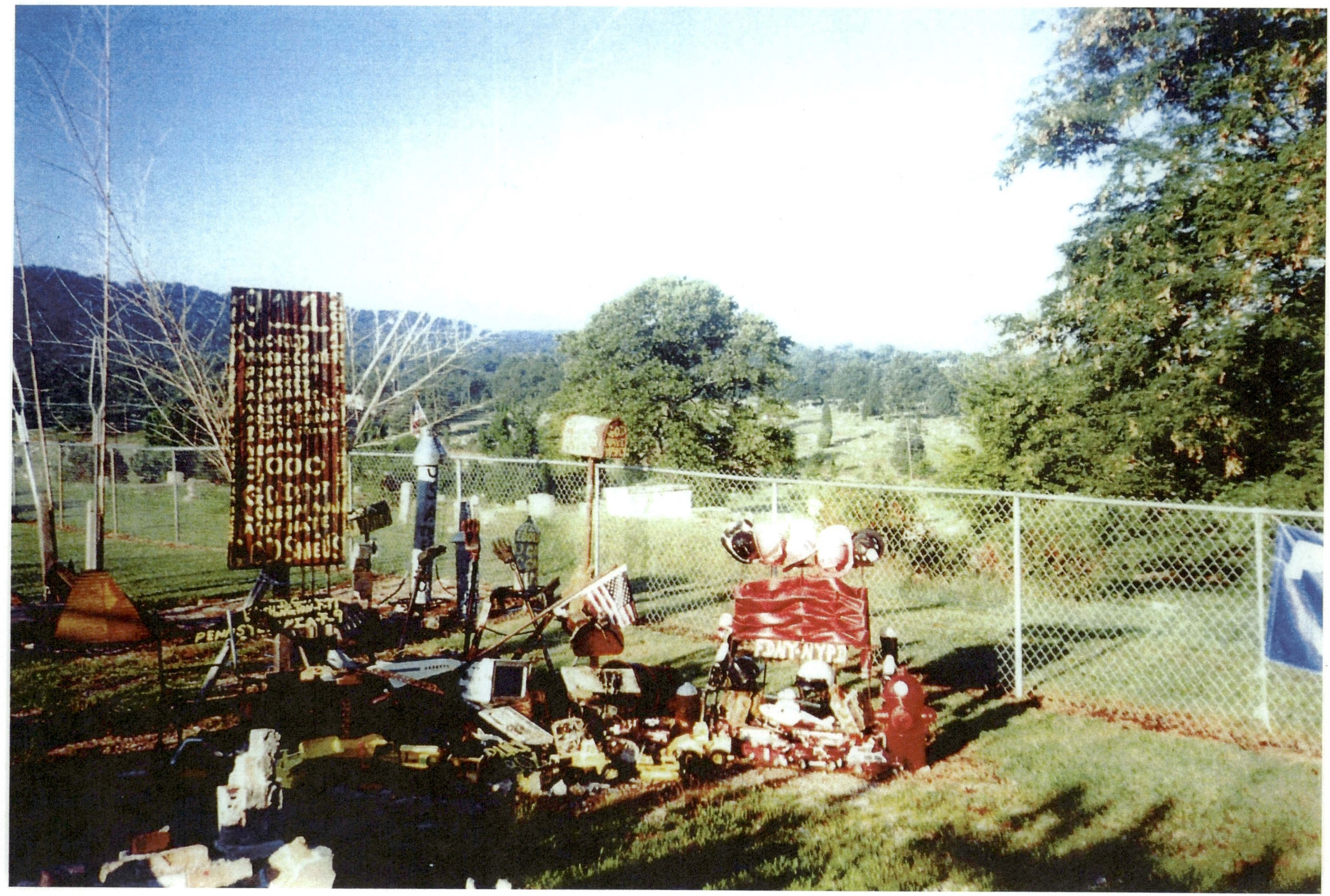
FDNY-NYPD

She told me that anything someone gives you is from the heart and do not be ashamed to take what they give you and thank God for it. The brother let me use his pen and he told me to keep the pen. I used it so I could write the end of this book. His pen ran out of ink on page 80, where I wrote God first for he is the Alpha and the Omega. After that I had to get another pen. The African Brother told me the size of the book he drew it on the ground and he also gave me what would come out of the book. It took me 26 years to pick up this pen again. After God sent the brother to me; I have always moved when God told me to move. At this point God told me to move and I am glad that I obeyed. I thank God and praise him for sending me this brother right on time. The pen was a *Paper Mate Write Brother's* medium point pen. The cover was black and the tip was black and the middle was white. Too hearts between the paper and mate air hole at point of pen. God used my hand to write this book. I could feel it in the way that the ink flowed onto the paper. This was a 5-in-1 Theme Book Wire-O-Bound with 150 sheets 10 ½" X 8," made by St. Regis Consumer products division paper company in Birmingham, Alabama, 35217. The

price was only $1.29 and I only paid $.79 cents for it back in 1979.

CHAPTER 10

NATURAL DISASTERS

Earthquake 2004 December 25

Tournament, South Asia, and Africa

Matthew 24:7

7 for nation shall rise against nation, kingdom against kingdom, and there shall be famines, pestilence earthquakes in divers places. Racism genocide you are your brothers keeper. God my pray stop all killing, drugs, guns and disrespect, open your children's eyes.

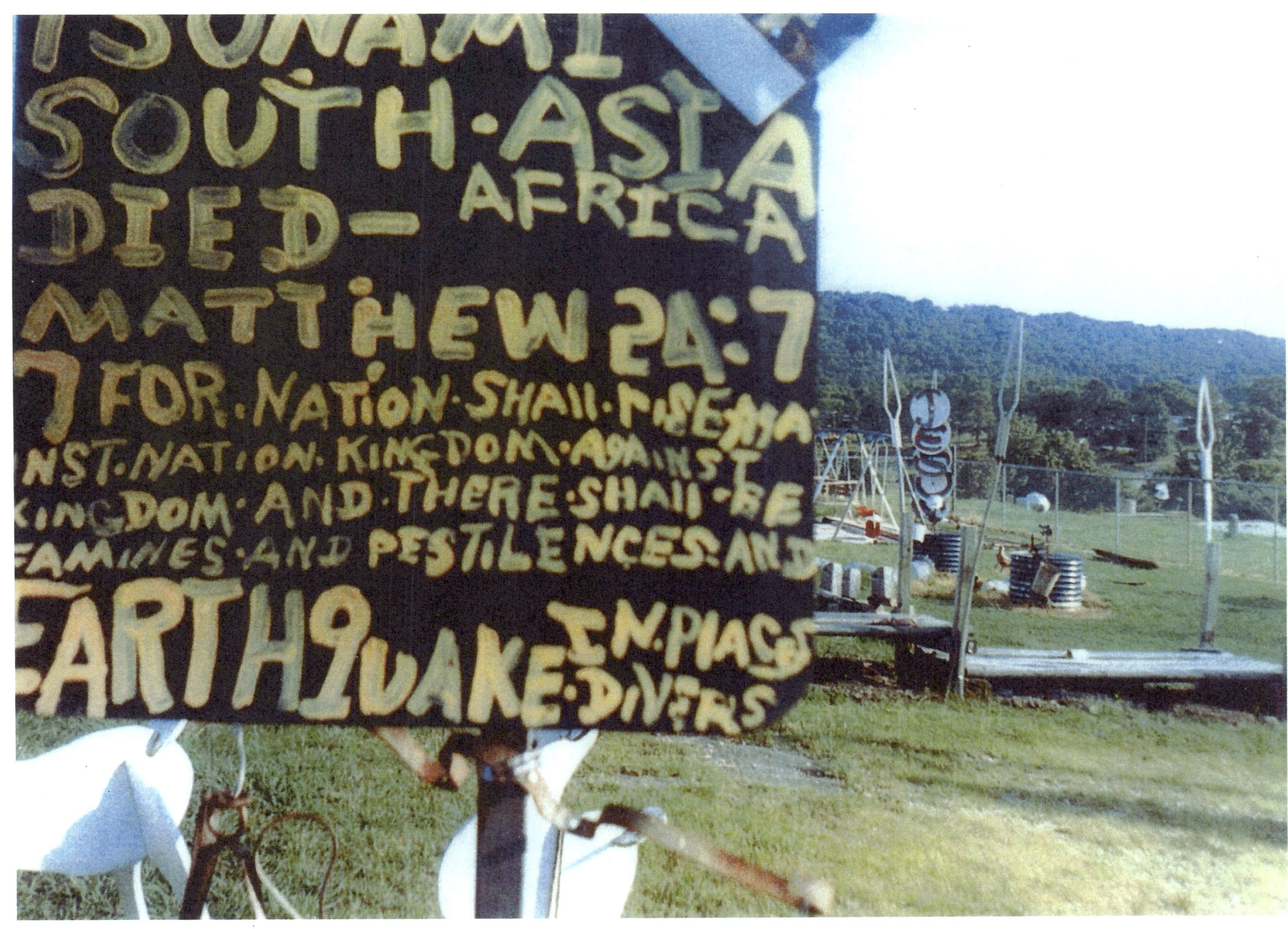
TSUNAMI
SOUTH·ASIA
DIED— AFRICA
MATTHEW 24:7
7 FOR·NATION·SHALL·RISE·AGA
NST·NATION·KINGDOM·AGAINST
KINGDOM·AND·THERE·SHALL·BE
FAMINES·AND·PESTILENCES·AND
EARTHQUAKE·IN·PLACES·DIVERS

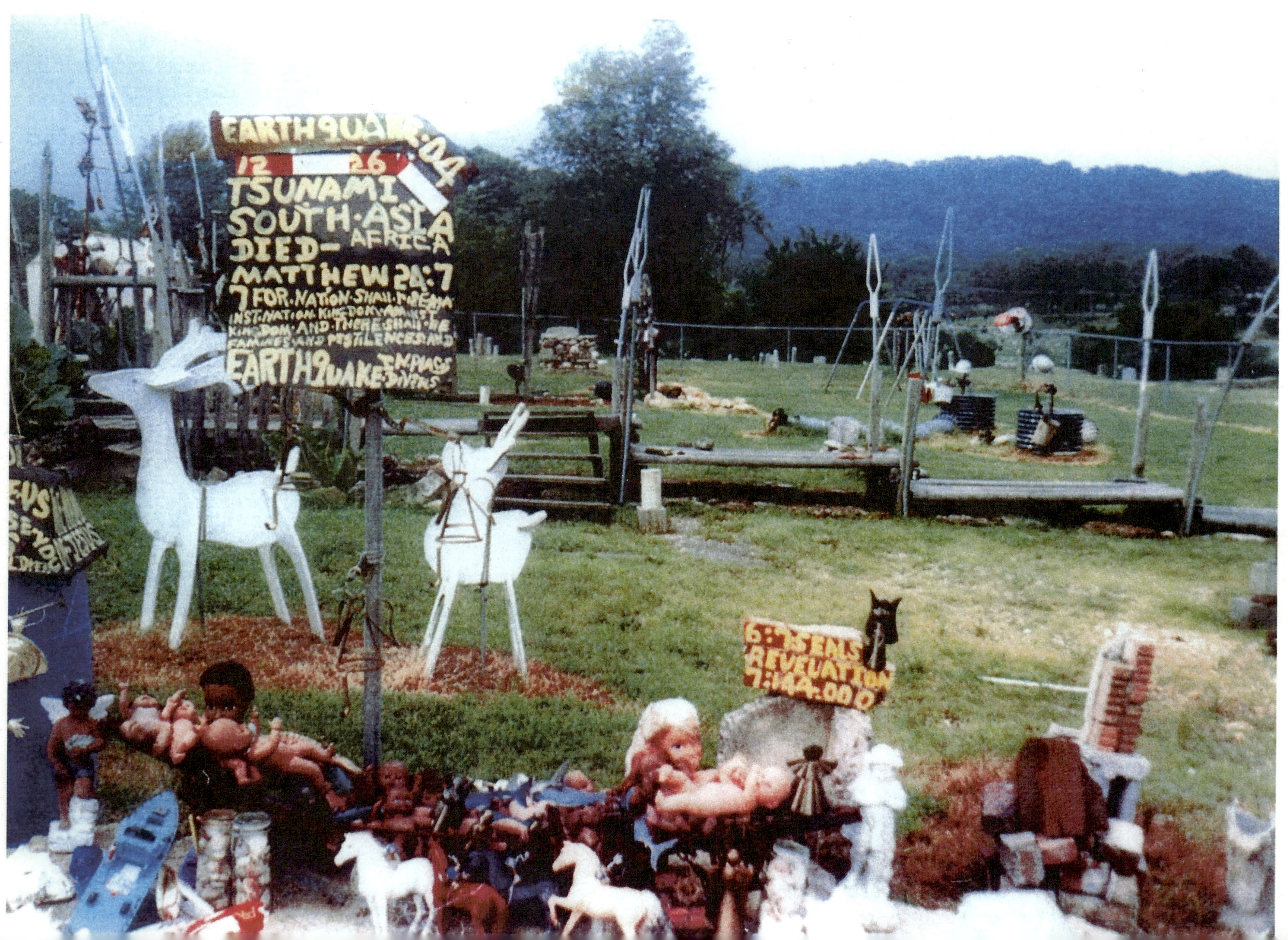

EARTHQUAKE '04
12 26
TSUNAMI
SOUTH ASIA
AFRICA
DIED -
MATTHEW 24:7
7 FOR NATION SHALL RISE AGAINST NATION, KINGDOM AGAINST KINGDOM AND THERE SHALL BE FAMINES AND PESTILENCES AND EARTHQUAKES IN DIVERS PLACES
6: 7 SEALS REVELATION 7:144,000 ?

TSUNAMI

REVELATION 6: 7 SEALS

7: 144,000 PEOPLE DEAD

GOD FORGIVE US. WE PRAISE YOU LORD SAVE THY CHILDREN IN THE NAME OF JESUS

TRIBULATION

ARMAGEDDON

REVELATION

1995

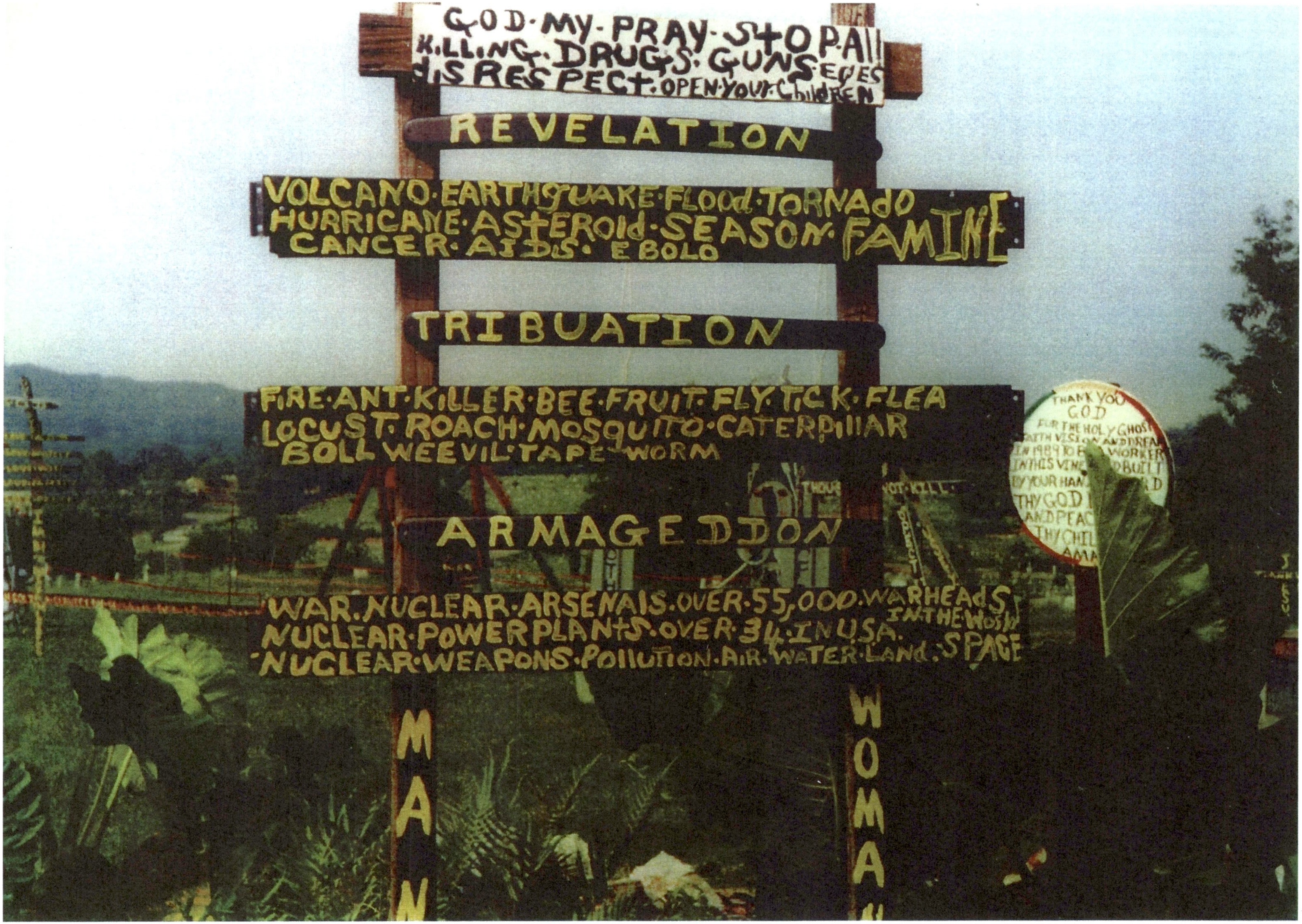

GOD·MY·PRAY·STOP·All
KILLING·DRUGS·GUNS EYES
disRESPECT·OPEN·YOUR·Children
REVELATION
VOLCANO·EARTHQUAKE·FlOOd·TORNAdO
HURRICANE·ASTEROID·SEASON·FAMINE
CANCER·AIDS·EBOLO
TRIBUATION
FIRE·ANT·KILLER·BEE·FRUIT·FLY·TICK·FLEA
LOCUST·ROACH·MOSQUITO·CATERPillAR
BOLL·WEEVIL·TAPE·WORM
ARMAGEDDON
WAR·NUCLEAR·ARSENAlS·OVER·55,000·WARHEAdS
INTHEWORld
NUCLEAR·POWERPLANTS·OVER·34·IN·USA·
·NUCLEAR·WEAPONS·PollUTION·AIR·WATER·LANd·SPACE
MAN
WOMAN
THANK YOU
GOD
FOR THE HOLY GHOST
FAITH VISION AND DREAM
IN 1989 TO BE A WORKER
IN THIS VINEYARD BUILT
BY YOUR HAND O LORD
THY GOD
AND PEACE
THY CHIL
AMA

Revelation

There will be volcanoes, earthquakes, floods, tornadoes, hurricanes, asteroids, season, cancer, aids, polio, droughts, famines, small pox, and anthrax.

Tribulation

Fire ants, killer bees, fruit flies, ticks, fleas, locust, roaches, mosquitoes, caterpillars, boll weevils, and tape worms.

Armageddon

There will be war, nuclear arsenals, and over 55,000 warheads, nuclear, power plants, and over 34 in the USA. Nuclear weapons, pollution, air, water, land, and space. Man, God forgive us. Woman God save us in the beginning.

To You Through me the Beginning of a Link of a journey of 400 years. God Love and Peace

Joe W. Minter

Peacemaker

God will judge us Birmingham Church U.S.A and the world for the treatment of our homeless brothers and sisters and children for they are God's children. We treat them like they are invisible because they are forced to live in boxes on the street and under the overpass in hot and freezing weather. We have destroyed their blankets, clothes, and medicine that were in Birmingham. They burned them up as they looked on and left them in the freezing weather and we call ourselves Christians. The which church in Birmingham, the United States, and the government can help our homeless Americans and give them a new look on life. God walks and talks with our homeless brothers and sisters and he tells them that he loves them also. This is because they are his children and he will never leave them alone.

Our Lord thy god we cast our burdens upon you for the lynching of all our African ancestors in the United States from 1555-2005. America needs to repent for we are in the last days. Amen. We have been made the invisible man here in America by the newspapers, television, radio, movies, and made to look like we are a people of crime or anything they want to portray us as. The African way is God, love, and peace. If you have a pie and you take out one slice out of it you only have a percent of what the whole pie is. Only the negative side of the contributions of the African to America portrayed there is a positive side of the African. African history has been robbed. Come into the African Community and give the real story and not just a slice of the pie, but the whole 100%.

Even though Africans have given America all they have to give, the true story of the conditions and the struggle of the African in America for 400 years had a chance to be exposed in 2001. In Durban, South Africa, to give the harm of racism and 400 years of slavery for the African in America and all of the free labor of the Africans to build America for 400 years. It is called reparations for the African. America was at the table of the whole world in Durban, South Africa with an opportunity given to America by God to repent. America got up from the table and walked out. A few days later September 11, 2001 occurred. How long can the Americans deny the Africans in America and what is due them? America is in the hands of God and only he can forgive and save them. May God have mercy on America?

REPENT

AMERICA

2005

<u>Jeremiah 23</u>

1 Woe be unto the pastors that destroy and scatter the sheep of my pasture saith the Lord.

2 Therefore this saith the Lord God of Israel against the pastors that feed my people; ye have scattered my flock and driven them away, and have not visited them. Behold, I will visit you on your doings, saith the Lord.

3 And I will gather the remnant of my flock out of all countries whither I have driven them, and will bring them again to their folds; and they shall be fruitful and increase.

4 And I will set up shepherds over them which shall feed them. They shall fear us no more, no be dismayed, neither shall they be lacking saith the Lord.

5 Behold the days come, saith the Lord, that I will raise unto David a righteous branch and a king shall reign and prosper, and shall execute judgment and justice in the earth.

6 In his days Judah shall be saved, and Israel shall dwell safely: and this is his name whereby he shall be called the Lord our righteousness.

7 Therefore, behold, the days come saith the Lord, that they shall no more say, the Lord liveth, which brought up the children of Israel out of the land of Egypt;

8 But, the Lord liveth which brought up and which led the seed of the house of Israel out of the north country and from all countries whither I had driven them; and they shall dwell in their own land.

9 Mine heart within me broken because of the prophets; all my bones shake; I am like a drunken man and like a man whom wine hath overcome, because of the Lord, and because of the words of his holiness.

10 For the land is full of adulterers; mourneth; the pleasant places of the wilderness and dried up and their course is evil, and their force is not right.

11 For both prophets and priests are profane, yea, in my house have I found their wickedness, saith the Lord.

12 Wherefore their way shall be unto them as slippery ways in the darkness; they shall be driven on, and fall therein: for I will bring evil upon them even the year of their visitation, saith the Lord.

13 And I have seen folly in the prophets of Samaria, they prophesied in Boal, and caused my people of Israel to evil.

14 I have seen also in the prophets of Jerusalem an horrible thing: they commit adultery, and walk in lies: they strengthen also the hands of evildoers that none doth return from his wickedness. They all of them unto me as Sodom, and the inhabitants there of as Gomorrah.

15 therefore thus saith the Lord of hosts concerning the prophets; behold, I will feed them with wormwood and make them drink the water of Gallilee: for from the prophets of Jerusalem is profaneness gone forth into all the land.

16 This saith the Lord of hosts, hearken not unto the words of the prophets that prophesy unto you; they make you vain: they speak a vision of their own heart, and not out of the mouth of the Lord.

17 They say still unto them that despise me, the Lord hath said ye shall have peace; and they say unto every on that walketh after the imagination of his own heart, no evil shall come upon you.

18 For who hath stood in the counsel of the Lord and hath perceived and heard his word? Who hath marked his word, and heard it?

19 Behold a whirlwind of the Lord is gone forth in fury, even a grievous whirlwind: it shall fall grievously upon the head of the wicked.

20 The anger of the Lord shall not return, until he have executed, and till he have performed the thoughts of his heart: in the latter days ye shall consider it perfectly.

21 I have not sent these prophets yet they ran: I have not spoken to them yet they prophesied.

22 But if they had stood in my counsel, and had caused my people to hear my word then they should have turned them from their evil way, and from the evil of their doings.

23 Am I a God at hand saith the Lord, and not a God afar off?

24 Can any hide himself in secret places that I shall not see him? Saith the Lord. Do not I fill heaven and earth? Saith the Lord.

25 I have heard what the prophets said, that prophesy lies in my name saying I have dreamed, I have dreamed.

26 How long shall this be in the heart of the prophets that prophesy lies? Yea, they are prophets of the deceit of their own heart.

27 Which think to cause my people to forget my name by their dreams which they tell every man to his neighbour, as their fathers have forgotten my name for Baal.

28 The prophet that hath a dream, let him tell a dream; and he that hath my word, let him speak my word faithfully. What is the Chaff to the Wheat? Saith the Lord.

29 Is not my word like as a fire? Saith the Lord; and like a hammer that breaketh the rock in pieces?

30 Therefore behold I am against the prophets, saith the Lord, that steal my words everyone from his neighbour.

31 Behold, I am against the prophets, saith the Lord that use their tongues, and say he saith.

32 Behold I am, against them that prophecy false dreams, saith the Lord, and do tell them, and cause my people to err by their lies and by their lightness; yet I sent them not nor commanded them: therefore they shall not profit this people at all saith the Lord.

33 And when this people or the prophet or a priest shall ask thee saying, what is the burden of the Lord? Thou shalt then say unto them, what burden? I will even forsake you, saith the Lord.

34 And as for the prophet and the priest, and the people, that shall say. The burden of the Lord, I will even punish that man and his house.

35 Thus shall ye say everyone to his neighbour, and everyone to his brother, what hath the Lord answered? And what hath the Lord spoken?

36 And the burden of the Lord shall ye mention no more for every man's word shall be his burden; for ye have perverted the words of the living God, of the Lord of hosts our God.

37 Thus shalt thou say to the prophet, what hath the Lord answered thee? And what hath the Lord spoken.

38 But since ye say, the burden of the Lord; therefore this saith the Lord; because ye say this word, the burden of the Lord, and I have sent unto you, saying, ye shall not say, the burden of the Lord;

39 Therefore, behold, I, even I, will utterly forget you, and the city that I gave you and your fathers, and cast you out of my presence:

40 And I will bring an everlasting reproach upon you, and a perpetual shame, which shall not be forgotten.

I Corinthians 13

Though I speak with the tongues of men and of angels, and have not charity, I am become as sounding brass, or a tinkling symbol.

2 And though I have the gift of prophecy, and understand all mysteries, and all knowledge; and though I have all faith, so that I could remove mountains, and have not charity, I am nothing.

3 And though I bestow all my goods to feed the poor, and though I give my body to be burned, and have not charity, it profiteth me nothing.

4 Charity suffereth long and is kind; charity evnvieth not; charity vaunteth not itself, is not puffed up.

5 Doth not behave itself unseemly, seeketh not her own, is not easily provoked, thinketh no evil;

6 Rejoiceth not in iniquity, but rejoiceth in the truth;

7 Beareth all thins believeth all things hopeth all things, endureth all things.

8 Charity never faileth: but whether there be prophecies, they shall fail; whether there be tongues they shall cease; whether there be knowledge, it shall vanish away.

9 For we know in part, and we prophesy in part.

10 But when that which is perfect is come, then that which is in part shall be done away.

11 When I was a child I spake as a child, I understood as a child, I thought as a child: but when I became a man, I put away childish things.

12 For now we see through a glass, darkly; but then face to face; now I know in part: but then shall I know even as also I am known.

13 And now abideth faith, hope, charity, these three; but the greatest of these is charity.

Jeremiah 30

The word that came to Jeremiah from the Lord, saying,

2 Thus speaketh the Lord God of Israel, saying, with thee all the words that I have spoken unto thee in a book.

3 For, lo the days come saith the Lord, that I will bring again the captivity of my people Israel and Judah, saith the Lord: and I will cause them to return to the land that I gave to their fathers, and they shall possess it.

4 And these are the words that the Lord spake concerning Israel and concerning Judah.

Chronicles 7

14 If my people, which are called by my name, shall humble themselves and pray, and seek my face, and turn from their wicked ways, then will I hear, from heaven, and will forgive their sin and will heal their land.

ONE NATION UNDER GOD

PRIDE, DISGRACE, AND SHAME

IN THE POWER TO KILL MEN
WOMEN, AND CHILDREN WITH
BOMBS RAINING DOWN FROM
THE SKY WITH NO MERCY, AND
NO COMPASSION....IN THE NAME
OF GOD NO!

IN USING THE   IN NOT OBEYING
LORD THY   GOD'S WORD TO
GOD'S NAME   LOVE THE LORD
IN VAIN   THY GOD WITH
ALL MIND AND SOUL
AND LOVE THY NEIGHBOR
AS THYSELF

IN THE POWER TO MAKE A LAW IN THE NAME OF GOD TO GIVE YOUR BROTHERS THE FREEDOM TO BE A MAN, GO BACK AND TO GO AGAINST GOD AND DESTROY THE LAW: HOW COULD GOD BE PLEASED WITH THIS?

IN THE POWER TO BUILD JAILS AND FILL THEM UP WITH YOUR BROTHERS WHILE YOU REMAIN FREE.

TO STRIP FROM YOUR BROTHER THAT WHICH GOD HAS GIVEN HIM AT HIS BIRTH: HOW COULD GOD BE PLEASED WITH THIS?

TO BREAK UP THE FAMILY OF YOUR BROTHER WHILE YOU HAVE THE FREEDOM TO LOVE YOUR FAMILY AND PROVIDE FOR THEM, HOW COULD GOD BE PLEASED WITH THIS EITHER?

WE WILL NOT MAKE IT WITHOUT THE WHOLE FAMILY AS ONE.

THE AFRICAN FARMER

The African in agriculture can be described as a farmer. God gave the African farmer the seed, the knowledge, wisdom, and understanding of the earth to call it his mother. It was also suppose to protect the earth from all the harm. It was suppose to be the caretaker of the earth, to live in harmony with all that he had created on earth in the beginning, grass the herb yielding seed, and the fruit tree yielding fruit after his kind, whose seed is in itself upon the earth and it was so. God gave the African the seasons when the seed was to be placed into the earth. When the African was taken from the mother land of Africa into slavery by America and Europe, he was used in agriculture of farming the hardest back-braking work that there is in the world. The Africans were placed in the hottest parts of America, the southern regions. They were expected to work in the hottest conditions from sun up to sundown 7 days a week. Overseers and plantation owners rode horses and carried whips to keep the slaves disciplined. The African farmer was forced to go fast without payment. They grew crops like cotton, rice, sugar cane, and tobacco. Many of the crops were cash making crops and the slaves were not given any form of payment whatsoever. Many of our ancestors worked until their deaths with no control over anything. They captured millions of our ancestors from the motherland of Africa. They were promised a lifetime of slavery without any benefits. The banks, government, insurance companies, and many other businesses made profits off of the back of our ancestors.

Sharecroppers were tenant farmers who shared the crops he grew with the owner of the land. This was a simple trick played on the slave. They still didn't get paid money. Their payment was being able to keep some of the crops that were no good and to live in a shack on the land never to own it for themselves. When the Africans went to the seed stores they were overcharged for the worst seed. The best seed were given to the whites and were less expensive. The white farmers always had the best land. Each year the African was told he could not gain ownership of the land he farmed undoubtedly all his life with his family. When his harvested his crops and took them to the mill to get his pay for the services they were always told they would do better the next year, but they still owed them for the current year because they did not farm enough crops. The African farmer had to fight the Ku Klux

Klan, the government, the land owners, and the bank without any positive results. There was no win for the African farmer in America or in Europe. He was never given an opportunity to succeed and when he did, he was told otherwise. Unfortunately God would be the one to feed the world the awful truth through knowledge, wisdom, and understanding. Look at what God gave Dr. George Washington Carver-chemist/agriculturist 1864-1943. He gave him the idea of new uses for agricultural products such as the peanut, sweet potatoes, and soybean. God revealed his knowledge, wisdom, and understanding to Dr. Carver and paved a path for him. He gave him an opportunity to help the entire world.

K K K

2005

TO YOU THROUGH ME: The Beginning of a Link of a Journey of 400 Years

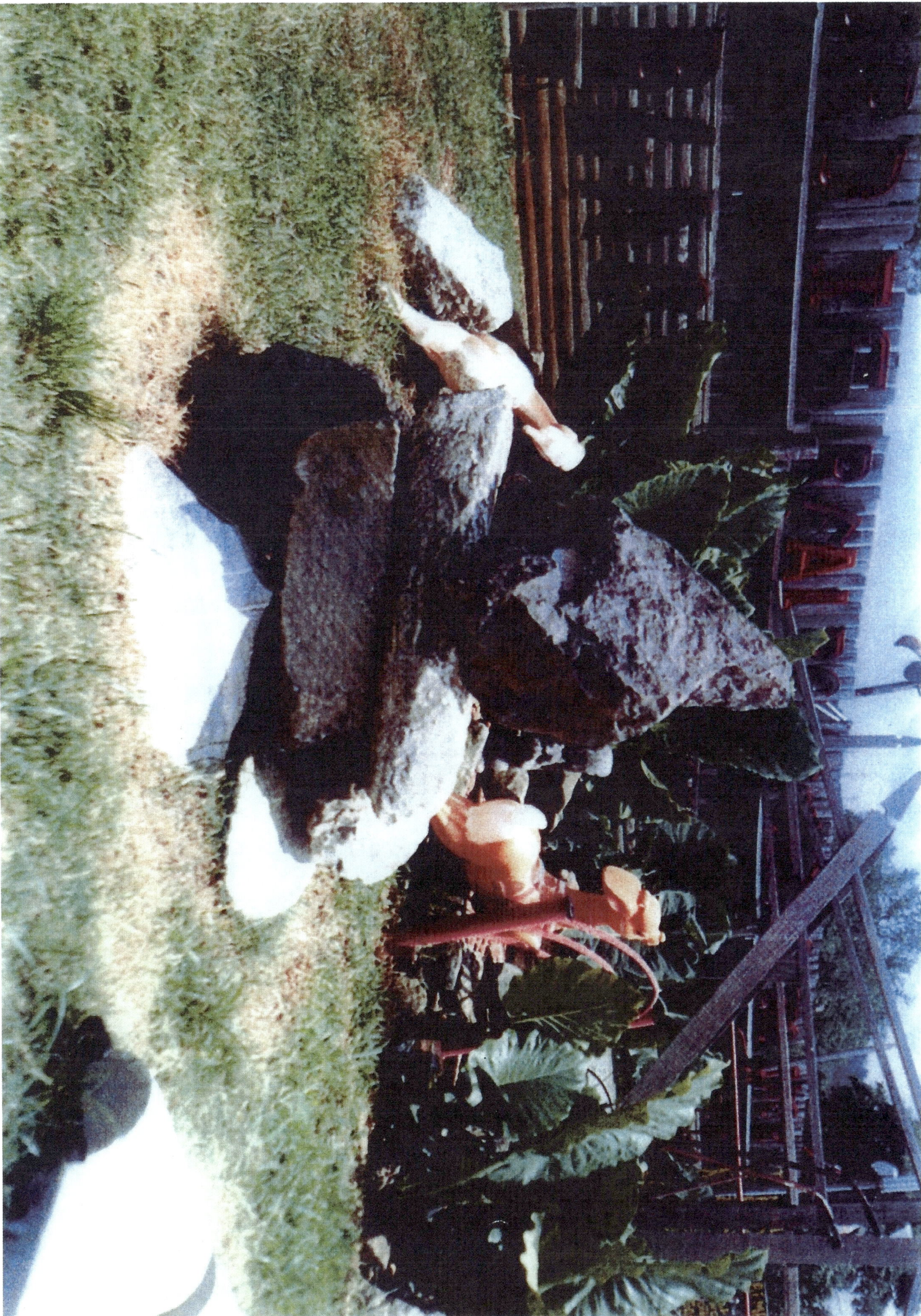

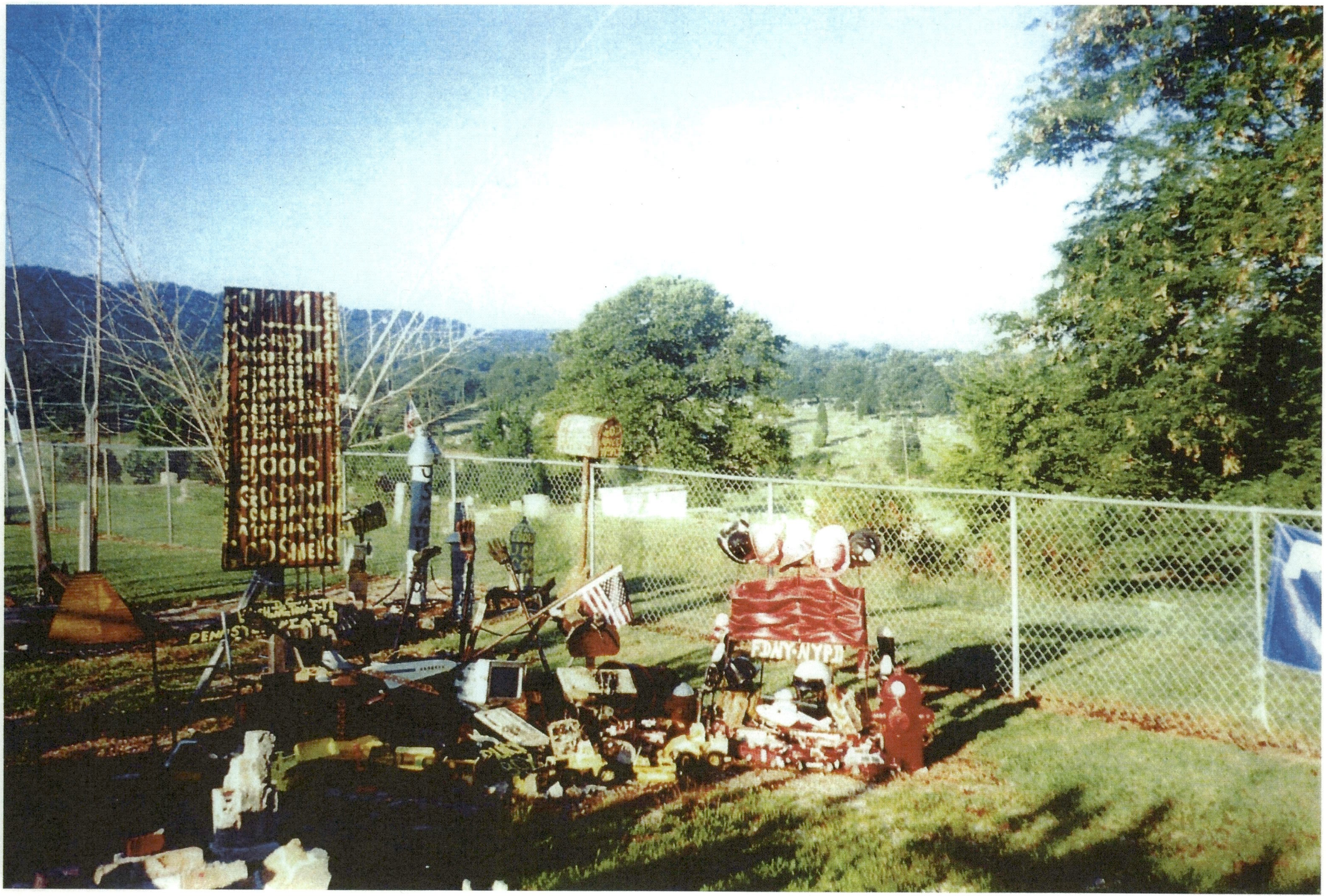
911
FDNY-NYPD
GOD SAVE US

The African Artist 2005

Genesis 1:1

In the beginning God created the heaven and the earth. Art is a gift from God to man for universal understanding. There is no inside or outside art, all of it is a gift from God to man. God was the first artist that ever existed.

Genesis 1:16

God made the great lights; the greater light to rule the day, and the lesser light to rule the night; he made the stars also.

Genesis 1:31

God saw everything that he made and behold it was very good. Thank you, God for the gift of art.

JEHOSHOPHATS'S PRAYER

2 Chronicles 20

12. Our God wilt thou not judge them? We have no might against this great company that cometh against us; neither know we what to do but our eyes are upon thee. God loves all of his children.

JABEZ PRAYER

1 Chronicles 10

10. And Jabez called on the God of Israel, saying, oh that thou wouldest bless me indeed, and enlarge my coast, and that thine hand might be with me, and that thou wouldest keep me from evil, that it may not grieve me! And God granted him that which he requested.

My prayer as an African artist and for all African artists all over your earth our Lord thy God is that. All artist come together in these last days as brothers and sisters in the name of Jesus as one to bring the whole earth together in the form of love for humanity to clean up the earth which we have just about destroyed. We must remove drugs, hate, hunger, homelessness, hurt, hostility and war. This is my prayer o Lord…that you open the door for the African artist to be able to tell his story because the world has made the African artist invisible and we have a 400 year story to tell of our middle passage and diaspora of being brought out of the great motherland of Africa. We have been brought out of freedom into the chains and shackles of slavery into the belly of many slave ships, lost freedom, misery, agony and death. It has been a 400 year journey. The African heart and the African way is God, love, and peace. Praise the Lord.

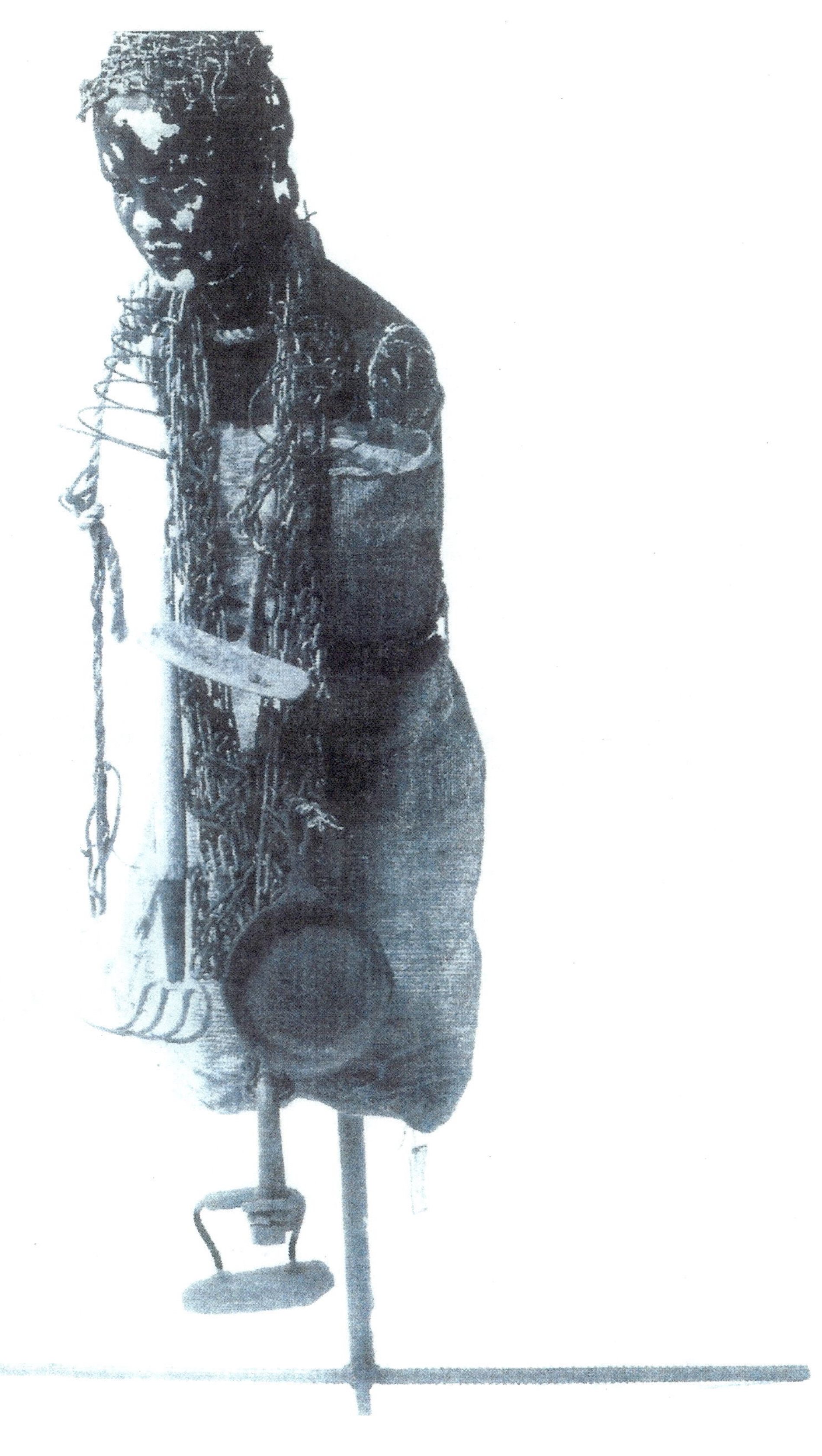

Right
Plate 1
Joe Minter
Where Is My Baby? 2001
Found materials
53 × 40 × 44"
(135 × 102 × 112 cm)

Stones suggest early modern behavior

By PAUL RECER
The Associated Press

WASHINGTON — Intricate patterns engraved on bits of stone found in a cave and dated at 77,000 years suggest ancient humans in Africa developed complex behavior and abstract thought thousands of years earlier than the famed cave painters of Europe.

Pieces of crafted ochre, a stone used for carving and for making pigment powder, were unearthed from the floor of a seaside cave in South Africa.

The find pushes back by some 35,000 years the earliest time when biologically modern humans were known to have developed modern behavior, said Christopher S. Henshilwood, first author of a study that appears Friday on *Sciencexpress*, the online version of the journal *Science*.

"The theory up until now has been that modern human behavior started only around 40,000 years ago," said Henshilwood, a researcher at State University of New York, Stony Brook, and at the Iziko Museum of Cape Town, South Africa.

Henshilwood said a list drawn up 30 years ago by archeologists suggested that the yardstick for modern behavior among ancient people should include evidence of the ability to produce art, such as cave paintings, to make bone tools, and to develop the fairly complex technology and organization needed to catch food, such as fish. Such factors would demonstrate that the ancient people had a modern ability to reason, to create, to organize and to plan.

Until now, it was believed that such behavior first appeared in Europe. Cave paintings and other artifacts showing advanced thought processes have

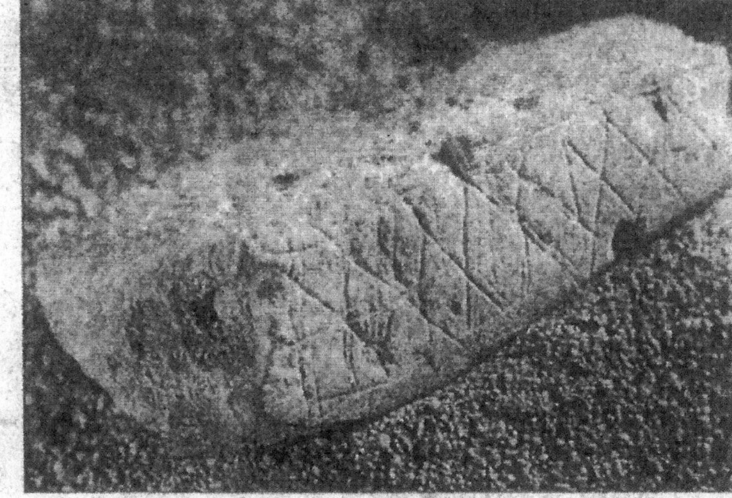

Etchings on this 77,000 year-old ochre stone, found in a seaside cave east of Cape Town, South Africa, suggest ancient humans were capable of complex behavior and abstract thought thousands of years earlier than once believed.

been uncovered at a number of sites in Europe.

But Henshilwood said discoveries in the Blombos Cave east of Cape Town on the Indian Ocean show that modern human behavior developed in Africa earlier.

He said the cave contains thousands of pieces of worked ochre, along with polished bone tools and many bones from fish — all signs of modern behavior.

On the Net
► *www.eurekalert.org*
► *www.sciencexpress.org*

WHERE IS MY BABY?

Genesis Chapter 2 Verse 22

And the rib, which the Lord God had taken from man, made he a woman, and brought her unto the man.
23 And Adam said, "this is now bone of my bones, and flesh of my flesh; she shall be called woman, because she was taken out of man".

We are all the babies of Eve. The African mother lost her babies in the mother land of Africa because of slavery as well as in America. The whole world knew her babies were taken away from her because of slavery. God gave me the vision and materials to give to the world the hurt of the African mother in the loss of her babies and her hurt that was done to her by slave labor. I could feel God moving my hands on each piece of art that I placed my hands on. It was made for the people of the world to see and feel the hurt of the African mother in the loss of her new babies. Jane Fonda took this piece of art as if she would share it with the world, yet has put it in her apartment. My prayer is that the whole world will get a chance to see this piece of art.

IRAQ FREEDOM 2003

GOD SAVE US

STOP THE BOMBING, AGONY, MISERY, OUR FEAR, & DEATH.

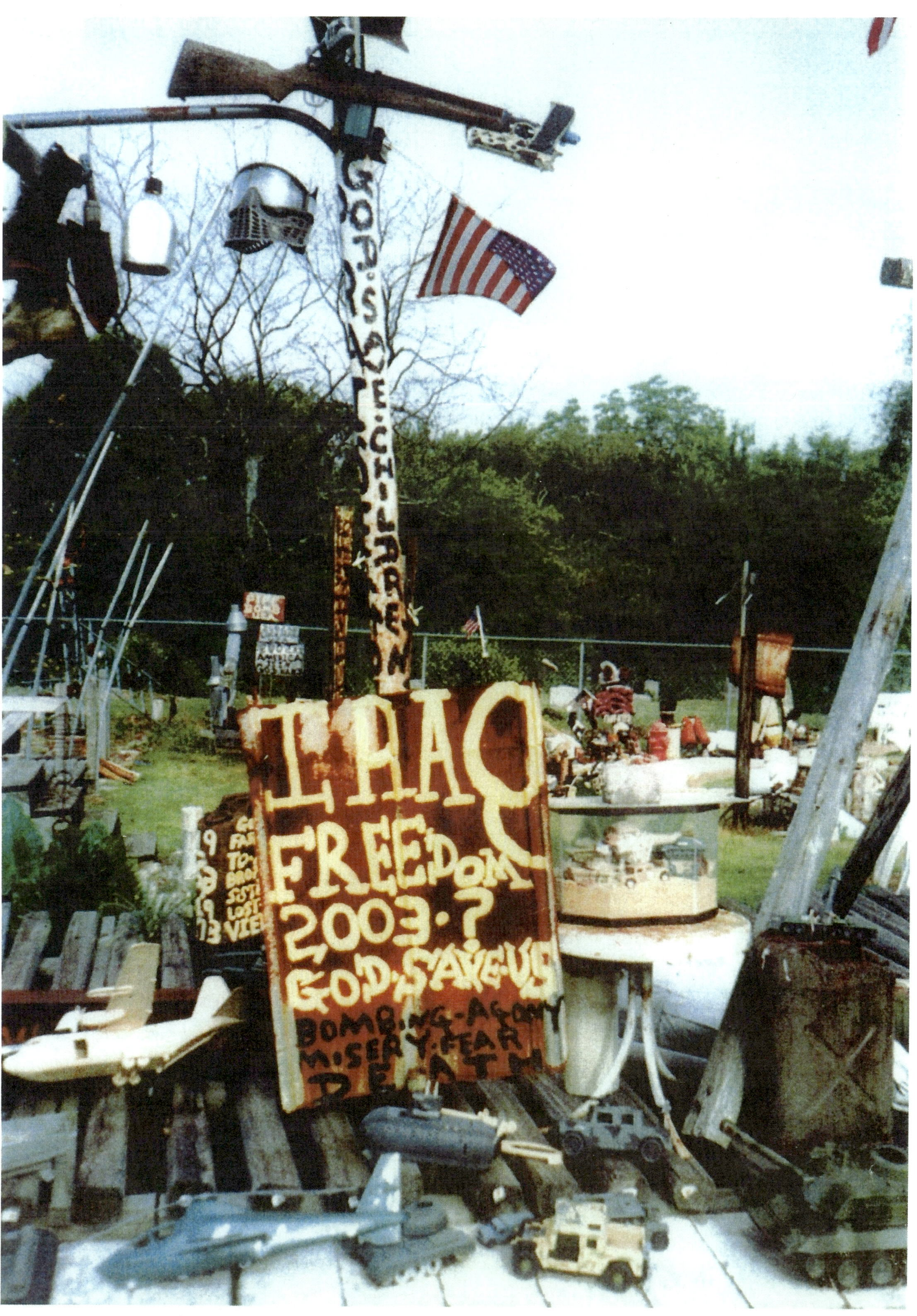
GOD·SAVE·CHILDREN
IRAQ
FREEDOM-
2003·?
GOD·SAVE·US
BOMBING·AGONY
MISERY·FEAR
DEATH

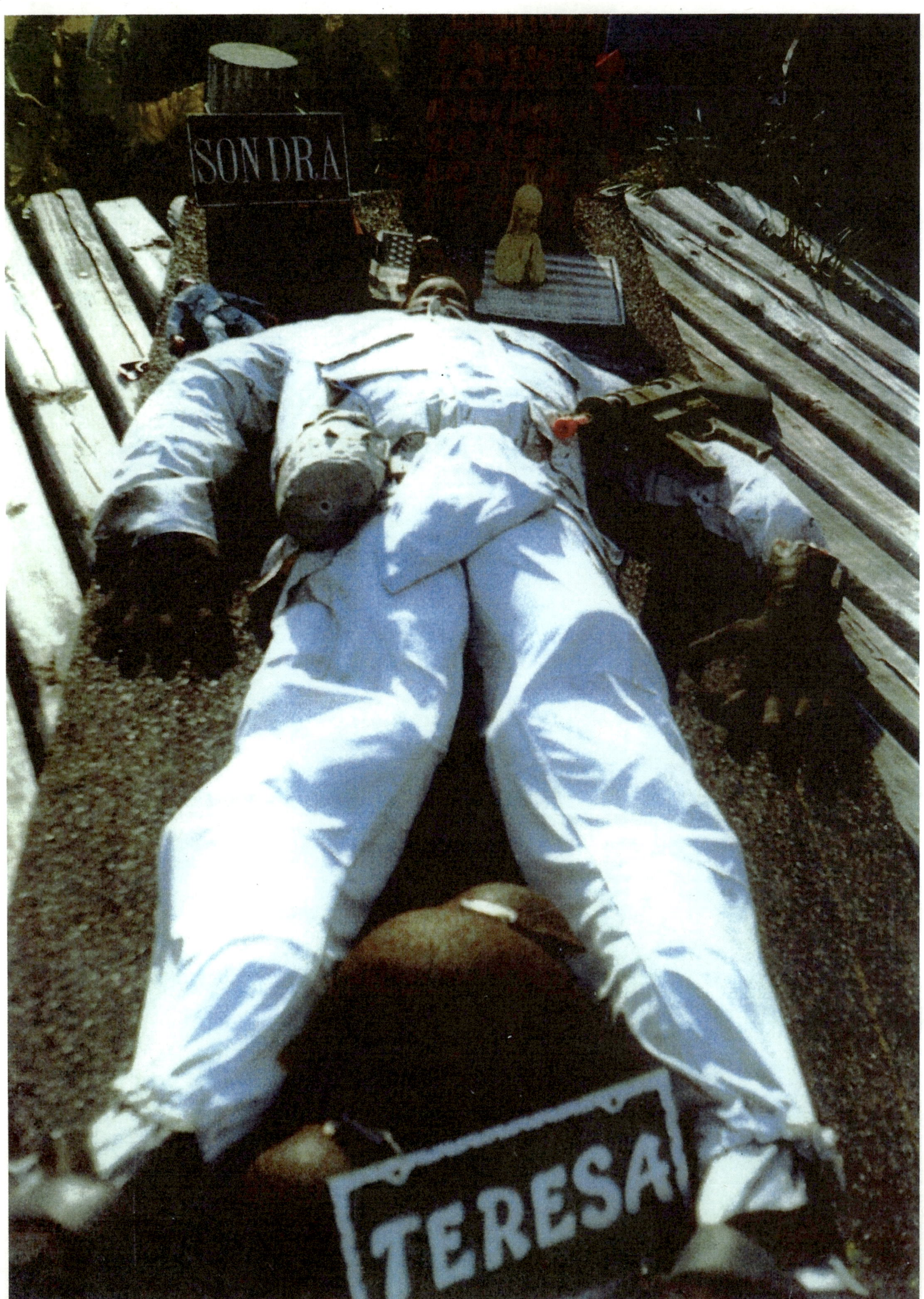

SONDRA
TERESA

THE BURDEN OF THE CROSS, THE CHAIN, THE ROPE, AND THE WHIP

THIS IS THE BURDEN OF THE CROSS, THE CHAIN, THE ROPE, THE WHIP, THE BURDEN OF SLAVERY, AND THE BURDEN OF FREE LABOR. GOD HAS BROUGHT HIS BELOVED AFRICAN CHILDREN ALL THIS WAY FOR MORE THAN 400 YEARS. HE WILL DELIVERED US ON TIME. KEEP YOUR HAND IN THE LORDS HAND. PRAISE THE LORD

THE ART HOUSE

THIS HOUSE WAS BUILT ABOUT OVER 60 YEARS AGO IN 1945.

PIECE BY PIECE HANDCRAFTED IN LOVE AND SWEAT BY AN

AFRICAN MAN WHO HAD TO LABOR HARD ALL DAY LONG AND

ALL NIGHT TO FINISH IT. GOD WAS WITH HIM. HE HAD TO DO THIS

FOR HIS FAMILY. THE HOUSE LOOKED GREAT UPON COMPLETION.

IN 2001, THIS HOUSE WAS STILL STANDING. NO ONE LIVES IN IT. IT

WAS IN BAD SHAPE WHEN WE BOUGHT IT. GOD PLACED IT IN OUR

HANDS. I DID THE BEST I COULD TO BRING IT BACK. TODAY, WE

USE IT AS AN ART HOUSE. GOD IS GOOD.

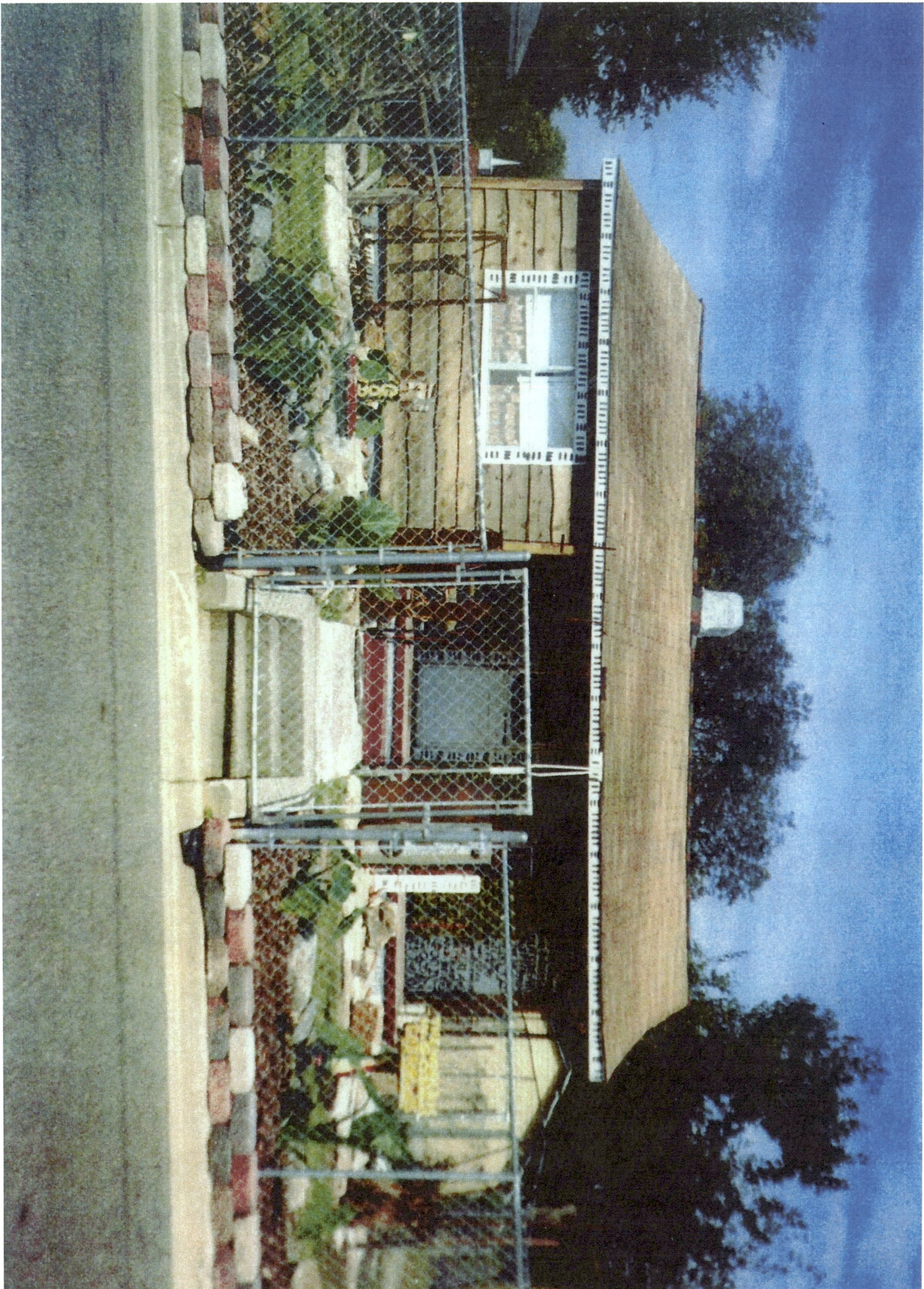

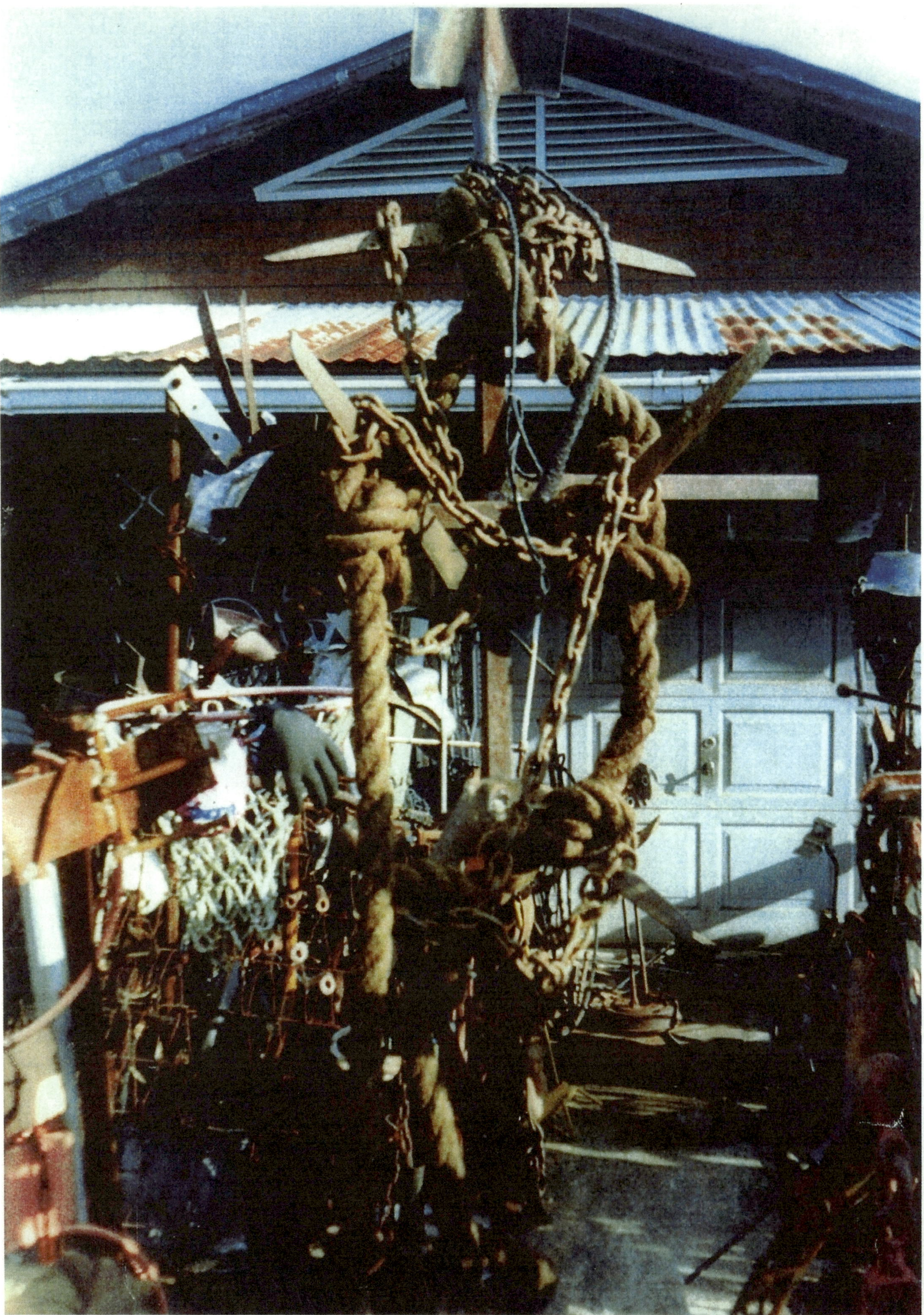

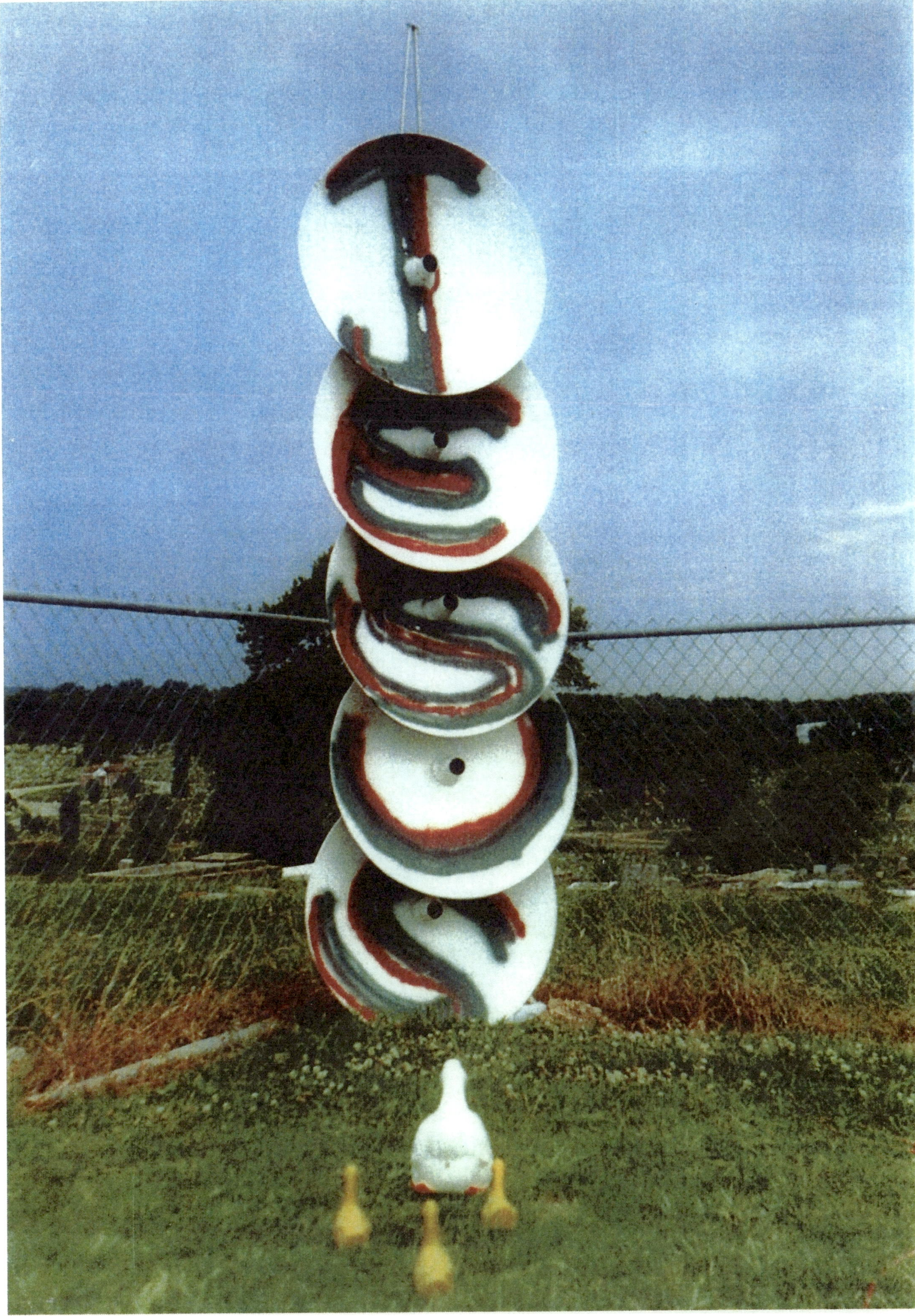

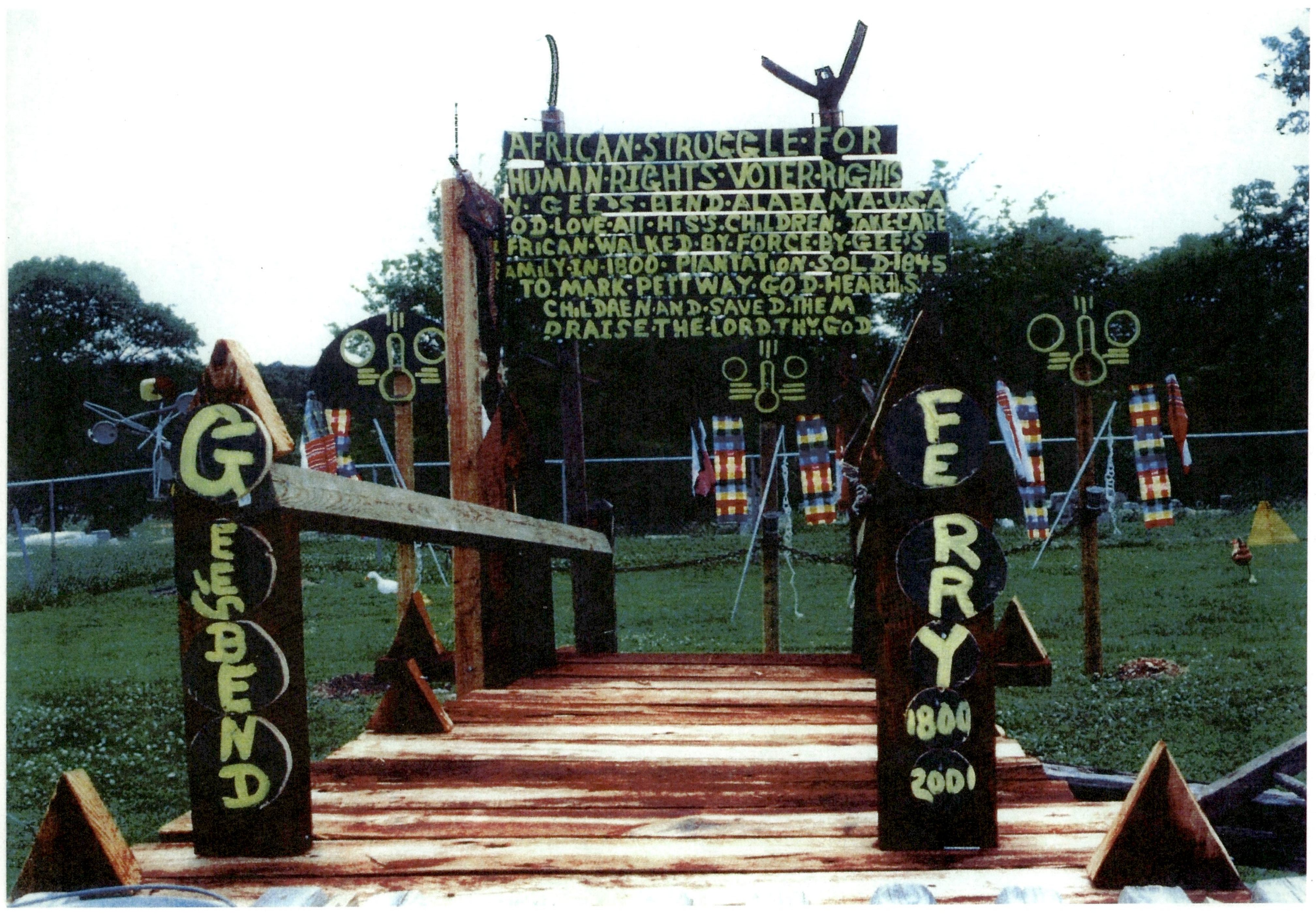
GEES BEND
FE RRY
1800
2001
AFRICAN STRUGGLE FOR
HUMAN RIGHTS VOTER RIGHTS
N. GEES BEND ALABAMA U.S.A
GOD LOVE ALL HISS CHILDREN TAKE CARE
AFRICAN WALKED BY FORCE BY GEES
FAMILY IN 1800 PLANTATION SOLD 1845
TO MARK PETTWAY GOD HEARTS
CHILDAEN AND SAVED THEM
PRAISE THE LORD THY GOD

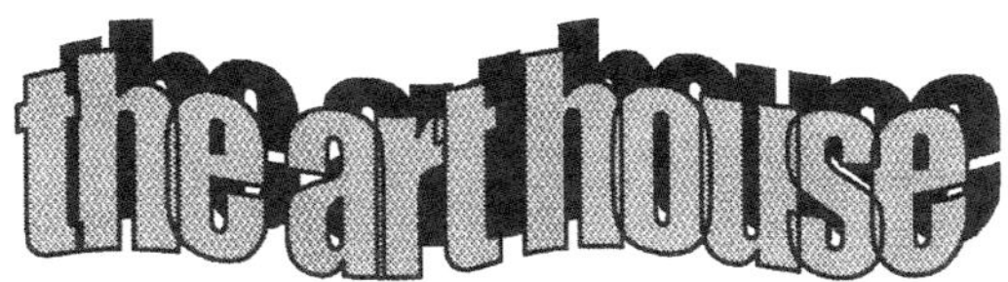

GEE'S BEND

THE AFRICAN MOTHER A LONG WAY FROM THE MOTHERLAND OF AFRICA WAS FORCED INTO SLAVERY. SHE HAD TO DEAL WITH THE LOSS OF HER GOD, HER CHILDREN, AND ALL OF HER AFRICAN SKILLS; SHE EVEN HAD TO DEAL WITH THE LOSS OF HER AFRICAN WAY OF LIFE.

SHE WAS FORCED TO WORK IN THE BIG HOUSE. AS SHE WORKED AT ONE OF HER MANY JOBS IN THE BIG HOUSE, QUILTING WAS MOST COMMON. SHE COULD SEE HER CHILDREN LAYING ON THE DIRT FLOOR IN THE SLAVE CABIN. SHE WOULD TAKE THE SMALL PIECES LEFT OVER FROM THE QUILT AND PUT THE PIECES IN HER POCKET. WHEN SHE ARRIVED AT HER CABIN LATE AT NIGHT, SHE WOULD SEW THE SMALL PIECES TOGETHER AS SHE LOOKED UPON HER CHILDREN SLEEPING PEACFULLY. A QUILT MADE BY HER HANDS IN LOVE TO GET HER CHILDREN OFF OF THE DIRT FLOOR ONE DAY. SOME OF THE HANDCRAFTED QUILTS WERE MADE FROM THE OLD CLOTHES HANDED DOWN FROM OTHER KINFOLKS.

SUMMARY

God give me the knowledge, wisdom and understanding, so that eyes can see me and ears can hear me touch the hearts of children, men, and women all over this earth. Give us heart to heart in these times that are near the end of the world, Lord we pray.

This book is a story of my life as an African descendent from African slaves on this side of the Atlantic Ocean. This is a long way from the motherland of Africa lost in America for 400 years. I was born here in America in on March 28, 1943. We did not have much but God took care of us as a family. I was blessed to have sweet and loving parents that protected and provided for us as their children. My father worked a hard job of a caretaker all of his life.   As an African American man he was denied the opportunity to be all he could be here in America. He worked himself to death and only received 4 social security checks before his death in 1959. My mother died in 2003.

This is also a story about my education, my jobs, and my contact with people…both black and white. It also summarizes the impact Jim Crow had on my life, how hate played such an astounding part of my teenage years, and how it felt to be made invisible in America because of the color of my skin. In 1979 I started writing this book and it wasn't until 2005 that I began to complete it. There has been change in America for Africans, but a lot of prejudice that exists today is swept under the rug, brushed off, and even ignored in order to keep peace. He is free by laws created, but is far from equal. He is still looked upon as a human being that is less than a Caucasian.

I asked God in 1989 to give me a vision and a mission to tell the story of the African people lost here in America. He told me art that is thrown away is similar to the African people thrown away here in America, and put his message with it not to ever stop working until I get his message out. Since 1989 I have worked 16 years on a park that I call the *African Village* in America. I made the art that carries the messages of those Africans that are lost here in America. God has given it wings and it has flown high above the clouds. Some people used the village to help themselves, but it is yet to reach the mess of people all over the world. I have been made invisible by the media and the people in power. All I want is to give the world the African version of what happened to us as we have become lost in America. May God give peace and understanding to those people who have the heart to read this book. May God bless and keep you.

A child of God
Joe Minter
Peacemaker
2005

IN THE

NAME OF

JESUS

2004

BIBLIOGRAPHY

THE HOLY BIBLE, KING JAMES VERSION

THE WORLD ALMANAC 1997 Volume Date

THE BIRMINGHAM NEWS volume. date year

STOLEN LEGACY BY G.G. JAMES

ALL AFRICA CONFERENCE OF CHURCHES ?

UNITED NATIONS GENERAL ASSEMBLY

CIVIL RIGHTS INSTITUTE BARRIERS GALLERY

PAUL AND WILLIAM ARNETT. **SOULS GROWN DEEP** VOLUME TWO

SHIRLEY GAVIN FLOYD. **THE FOOT SOLDIER INFORMER**

VIVIAN SAMMONS, **BLACKS IN SCIENCE AND MEDICINE**

ALL PHOTOGRAPHS AND WORKS OF ART ARE ALL CREATED BY JOE MINTER SR.

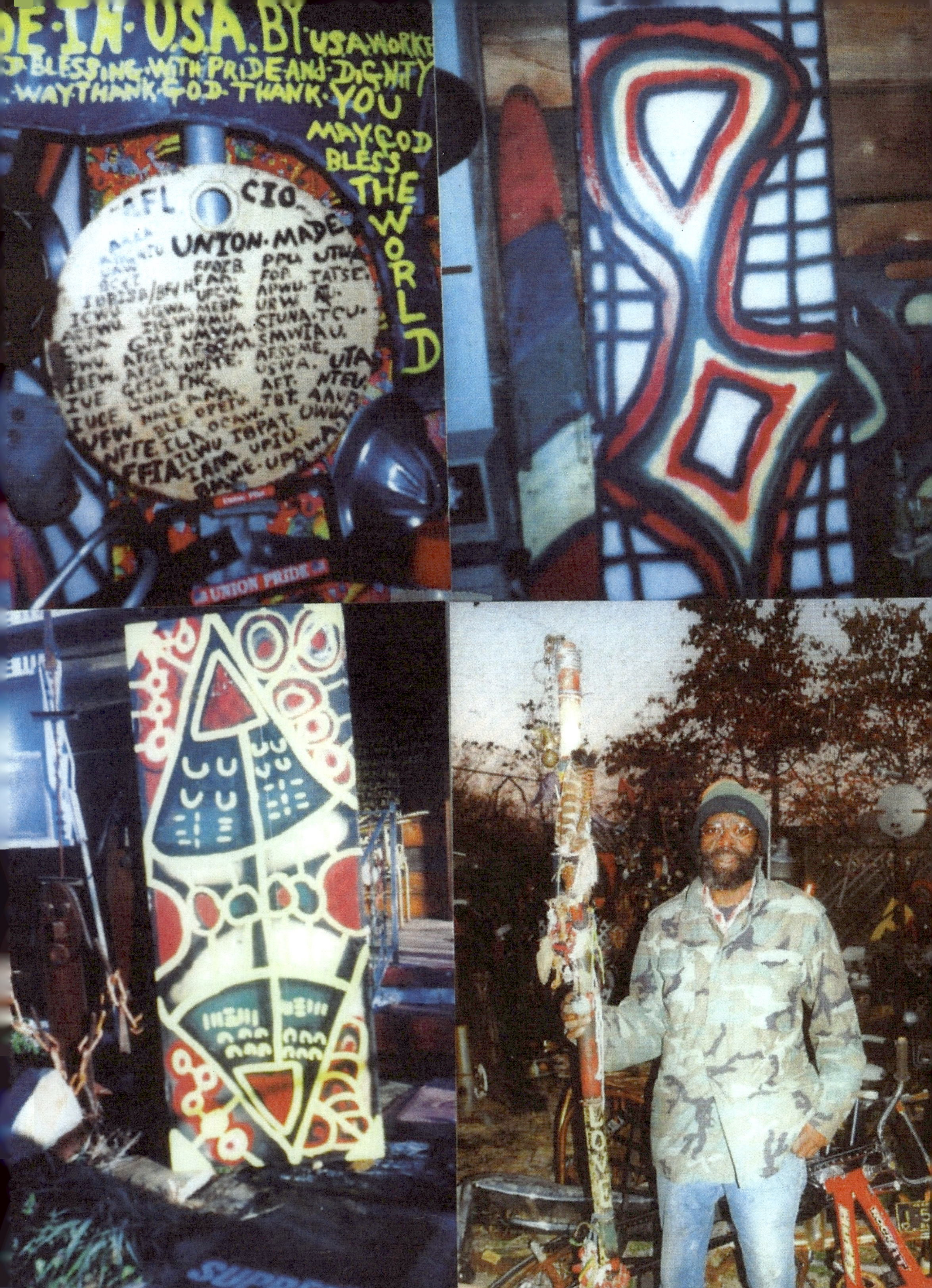
DE·IN·USA·BY·USA·WORKER
BLESSING·WITH·PRIDE·AND·DIGNITY
WAY·THANK·GOD·THANK·YOU
MAY·GOD·BLESS·THE·WORLD
AFL CIO
UNION·MADE
UNION PRIDE

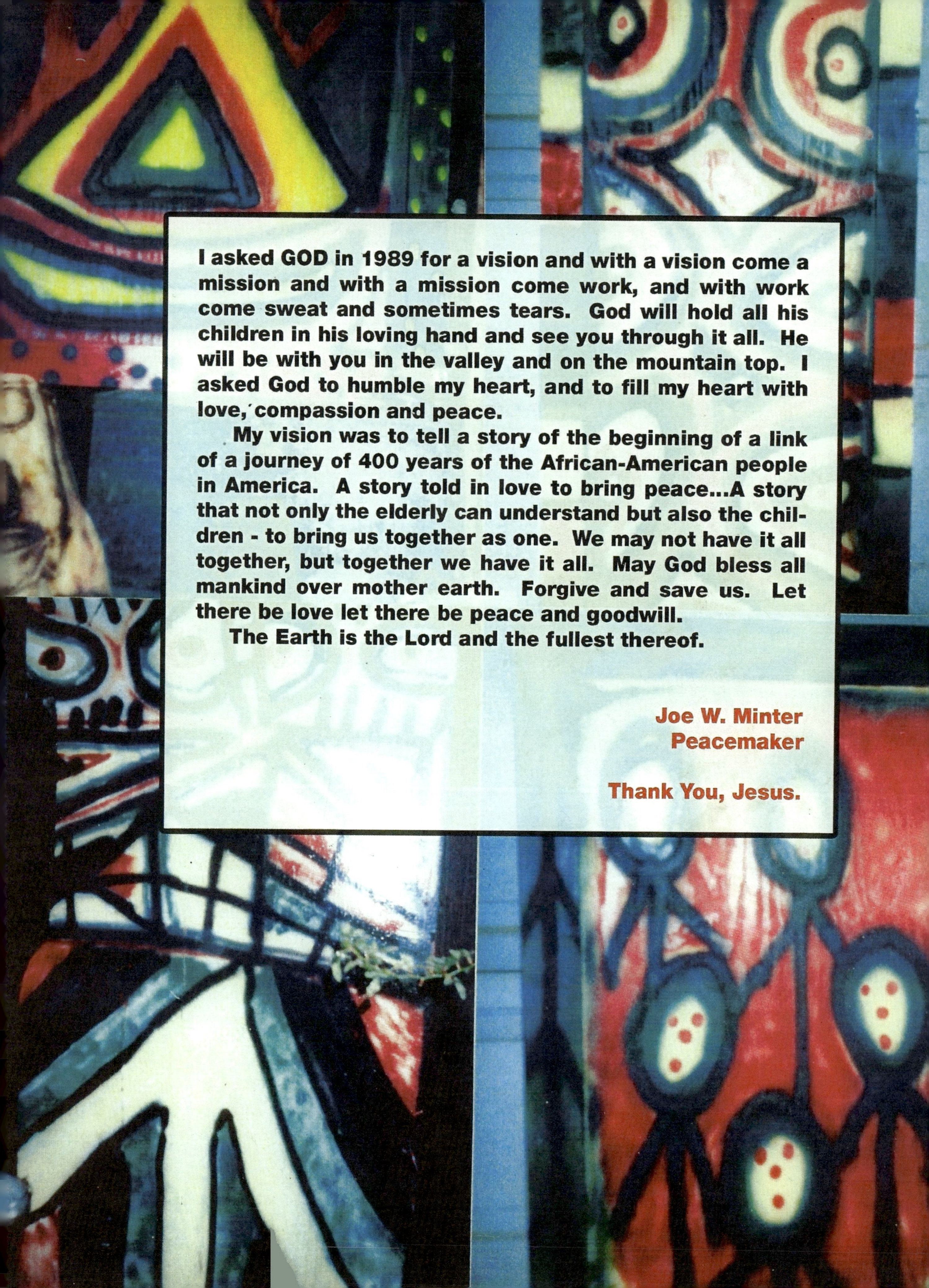

I asked GOD in 1989 for a vision and with a vision come a mission and with a mission come work, and with work come sweat and sometimes tears. God will hold all his children in his loving hand and see you through it all. He will be with you in the valley and on the mountain top. I asked God to humble my heart, and to fill my heart with love, compassion and peace.

My vision was to tell a story of the beginning of a link of a journey of 400 years of the African-American people in America. A story told in love to bring peace...A story that not only the elderly can understand but also the children - to bring us together as one. We may not have it all together, but together we have it all. May God bless all mankind over mother earth. Forgive and save us. Let there be love let there be peace and goodwill.

The Earth is the Lord and the fullest thereof.

Joe W. Minter
Peacemaker

Thank You, Jesus.